What Experts are Saying About *Dear Beautiful*

"A talented writer and prolific researcher, Dr. Gail Thompson speaks to African American women in search of their true identities. Gail does an amazing job helping us learn how to resist self-admonishments and narratives that create distorted images of our inner and outer selves. Drawing from research that elucidates the mental and emotional benefits of journaling, Gail takes the reader on a voyage of self-examination that is both cathartic and empowering. Dear Beautiful! is a 'must read' for women, especially African American women, who have allowed the media and cultural mores to define them."
M. Jean Peacock, Ph.D.
Professor of Psychology, Emeritus
Coordinator University Faculty Mentoring Network, CSUSB

"As an Assistant Principal at two elementary schools in Southern California, I deal with situations that cause an immense amount of stress from time to time. I love what I do, but there are times when I need to take the time to meditate and 'shut down.' Reading Dear Beautiful helps me unwind and remember why I do what I do. Best of all, I have things that I can share with the parents and students I work with who may need to remember that their beauty lies within. Gail's advice and the stories she shares reminds us all that we are all HUMAN and that we need to look beyond the mirror."
Nicole Moshiri, Ph.D. Elementary School Assistant Principal

"What an inspirational and bold way to address women of color, as we struggle with our skin tones, our kinky hair and our passionate every day conversation. Dear Beautiful is providing a road map for the Black Woman to be empowered. We are all in for an awakening. Dr. Thompson has challenged us to wake up, and embrace our inner and outer beauty."
Talisa A. Sullivan, Ph.D.
Lead Consultant, Transformational Leadership Consulting "TLC" Services, Inc.

"Right on target! Ladies, we too need to be reassured that our black is indeed beautiful! Dear Beautiful does exactly that. Dr. Gail's stories are our stories and her strategies will reaffirm our beauty, strength, and relevance! Dear Beautiful is much needed in our culture." **Leontye L. Lewis, Ed. D.**

What Experts are Saying About *Dear Beautiful* continued

"Dear Beautiful's essence provides valuable lessons on beauty, empowerment, and positive affirmations, and how to apply them in our daily lives. It captures the heart of Black girls' and women's desires to look and feel beautiful. The topics Dr. Gail Thompson addresses are relevant and necessary to continue to build our self-esteem, self-confidence, and bring inner peace to our spirits. We need this book, as it serves as a daily refresher of encouragement for all of us to look at ourselves, inwardly and outwardly, and serves to strengthen our souls. Simply inspirational!"

Dr. Angela Louque, Professor & Chair, Educational Leadership and Technology, CSUSB; co-author of *Exposing the Culture of Arrogance in the Academy: A Blueprint for Increasing Black Faculty Satisfaction*

"Do you know you are beautiful? Dr. Gail Thompson's latest book treats this question as a fact, and it is sure to inspire today's modern women and girls — especially African Americans. The book debunks popular myths and assumptions of Black womanhood as it provides a satisfying mix of affirmations, therapeutic art activities, and exercises to encourage self-reflection. Dr. Thompson's relatable personal stories make the book read like a warm and loving conversation with a dear friend. Dear Beautiful! is a much-needed contribution to Black American culture that should be shared with our friends, our mothers, our sisters, and especially our daughters."

TreaAndrea M. Russworm, Ph.D.
Associate Professor, UMass Amherst Department of English
Author: *Blackness is Burning: Civil Rights, Popular Culture, and the Problem of Recognition*; co-editor *From Madea to Media Mogul: Theorizing Tyler Perry*; and *Gaming Representation: Race, Gender, and Sexuality in Video Games*

"In Dear Beautiful, Dr. Thompson goes behind the veil and invites readers to remove the masks that have long covered the scars of hurt and isolation that so many have experienced. This resource is directive, empowering and uplifting. The journey to deep healing and the recognition of the jewels that we each carry (inward and outward) can be a challenging process, but it is highly necessary. If you are willing to spend a little time devoting yourself to reframing the tales that you have believed for so long, into the truths that are waiting to be embraced, I am confident that you will be blessed. I know that I am."

Tiffany S. Powell, Ph.D.
Project Manager, Teacher Professional Development, Center of Initiatives for Pre-College Education (CIPCE); Renessalear Polytechnic Institute, Troy, NY

Dear Beautiful! (Vol. 1)
A Self-Empowerment Book
For Black Women

Gail L. Thompson, Ph.D.

Contents

Part One: The Outside-- Looks, Likes, and Physical Appearance

Part Two: The Inside--True Beauty

Additional Books by Dr. Thompson

A Brighter Day: How Parents Can Help African American Youth

The Power of One: How You Can Help or Harm African American Students

Up Where We Belong: Helping African American and Latino Students Rise in School and in Life

African American Teens Discuss Their Schooling Experiences

What African American Parents Want Educators to Know

Through Ebony Eyes: What Teachers Need to Know but are Afraid to Ask About African American Students

Yes, You Can! Advice for Teachers Who Want a Great Start and a Great Finish with Their Students of Color (co-authored with Mr. Rufus Thompson)

Exposing the Culture of Arrogance in the Academy: A Blueprint for Increasing Black Faculty Satisfaction (co-authored with Dr. Angela Louque)

Reaching the Mountaintop of the Academy: Personal Narratives, Advice and Strategies From Black Distinguished and Endowed Professors (co-edited with Dr. Chance Lewis and Dr. Fred Bonner ll).

About the Author

Website: www.drgailthompson.com

Dr. Gail L. Thompson is a researcher, author, Equity and Professional Development Expert, and motivational speaker. During her time as the Wells Fargo Endowed Professor of Education at Fayetteville State University, she created and served as Director of the Black Men Teaching (BMT) Program, and supervised doctoral students.

Dr. Thompson has written chapters that were published in several edited books, an article that was published in USA, has served as a co-host of the radio program "Elevate," and has been a guest on PBS television's Tony Brown's Journal, as well as other television shows, and many radio programs.

Dr. Thompson is married to Rufus, a retired educator, author, Implementation Manager for Illuminate Education, and pilot. They have three adult children, Dr. Nafissa Thompson-Spires, a critically acclaimed author and university instructor; NaChe', a high school teacher, entrepreneur and inventor of Noki; and Stephen, a Mechanical Engineer and music composer. They are also the very proud grandparents of Iveren and Isaiah.

Acknowledgements

I thank God for giving me the vision to create a self-empowerment series. I also appreciate the support and encouragement of my husband and best friend of more than 31 years, Rufus Thompson. Rufus was the first person to suggest that I write this book, and he helped with formatting the book, designing the cover, scanning the drawings, etc. My adult children, Dr. Nafissa Thompson-Spires, Ms. NaChe' Thompson (who also proofread this book), and Mr. Stephen Thompson, son-in-law Dr. Derrick Spires, and my sister Mrs. Tracy Harkless (who also proofread this book and gave it "two thumbs up") were also very supportive.

I'm also grateful to Ms. Gloria Porter for her support, prayers, and encouragement for more than three decades, and for urging me to move forward with this project asap. Thanks also to Mother Gaynella Ewings for taking me to church during my childhood; Mother Myrtle Smith for praying for me throughout the years; Attorney Bettye Coleman for her friendship and prayers throughout the years; my cousin-friend Debbie Jo Crear; mother Velma Coleman; and my "cheering section" for this project: award-nominated author Dr. Jenny Grant-Rankin, my best friend from childhood, Mrs. Wanda Foster (for continuing to encourage me to write my story), Mrs. Elaine Richardson, Dr. Angela Louque, Ms. Cynthia Hebron, Mrs. Sharon Holmes-Johnson, Mrs. Susan Toler-Carr, and Mrs. Jocelyn Mixon, for their enthusiasm about this project.

I'm very grateful to the phenomenal Black women experts who agreed to endorse this book on short notice during the busy 2017 holiday season. These experts--Attorney Marilyn Quail, Dr. Leontye Lewis, Dr. Gina Newton, Dr. Tiffany Powell, Dr. Jean Peacock, Dr. Nicole Moshiri, Dr. Talisa Sullivan, Dr. Angela Louque, and my niece, Dr. TreaAndrea Russworm (who is also the author of several books) -- have been a huge blessing to me.

Illuminate Education Founder & former CEO, Mr. Lane Rankin who reminded me to pursue my passion, and many of my Illuminate Education coworkers--such as the accomplished artist Ms. Katya Mocalis, Mrs. Elena Seward, Mrs. Kristin Town, Mrs. Debra Russell, Mrs. Leilani Carbonell-Pedroni, Mr. Baxter Mante, Mr. Martin Yan, Mr. Joseph Bonifacio, and Ms. Tanya Phillips--gave me some much-needed wonderful compliments about this project. Mrs. Judy O. Hicks encouraged me to continue to be a "strong woman" within and outside of Corporate America. If I forgot to acknowledge *your* input and encouragement, please forgive me!

A Special Invitation

Dear Beautiful!

   I am very interested in learning how *Dear Beautiful!* has impacted you. Please email your comments and suggestions to me at **gailLt@aol.com**.

Introduction

Dear Beautiful!

This self-empowerment book is the first in a series that I plan to create. As the title states, this particular book is designed to help Black women become their best selves, especially by learning to accept, appreciate, and love their *inner* and *outer beauty*.

Dear Beautiful! contains:

- self-empowerment Journaling-Personal Growth Exercises
- self-image and self-esteem-building Daily Affirmations
- Art Therapy in the form of drawings for you to color and templates for you to create your own drawings
- lots of stories, including some about my life,
- important Life Lessons, and
- research, advice, and recommendations to help you identify your purpose, and develop your own "Roadmap to Success"

Art Therapy

For decades, many therapists have been using Art Therapy--the use of music, drawing, painting, etc.--to help children and teens recover from trauma. However, anyone can use art to improve her life. Regardless of age, most people enjoy listening to, humming, or singing their favorite songs, because music makes us feel better. The same is true of drawing. In meetings, classrooms, waiting rooms or other places, we may find ourselves "doodling," or drawing random objects, because this helps us pass the time. In recent years, the "adult coloring book" industry has grown tremendously, because many adults have realized that drawing and coloring are just as fun and relaxing today, as they were when they were children.

Two years ago, I began to purchase some of these adult coloring books--mostly ones consisting of flowers and landscapes, and I loved decorating them with colored pencils. Not only did I enjoy creating my own masterpieces, but I found coloring to be a great way to relax at the end of a busy day. In other words, "It was therapeutic."

One day, during a conversation with my husband, Rufus, a "lightbulb" went off in my head, and I decided that I should create my own self-empowerment and coloring book series for three main reasons. First, as an individual who has devoted my professional career to empowering others through my motivational speaking, professional development presentations, workshops, teaching, and writing, this series would be a great way for me to continue to empower others. Second, since childhood, drawing paper dolls and little Black girls, and painting them with watercolors, have been two of my favorite hobbies. Third, creating this series would be a great way for me to combine my writing, empowerment, and drawing talents.

With this in mind, I hope that you will use *Dear Beautiful!* to improve your life. If this happens, that means that I will have succeeded in reaching my goal: inspiring you to become your best self and owning your God-given *inner* and *outer beauty.*

Part One
The Outside:
Looks, Likes, and Physical Appearance

Chapter One
Physical Appearance and Internalized Messages

Dear Beautiful!

Long ago, when I was an 18-year-old college student, I knew another student--an African American teenager--who believed that Black women were cursed. Although we saw each other every day, this woman and I weren't friends. However, I often heard her tell other African American women, "Black women are cursed!" And whenever they tried to change her mind, this dark-skinned young woman would argue that she was right and they were wrong. Unfortunately, negative messages from the media, her childhood, and other sources had convinced her that this was true, and no one could change her mind.

But over time, this woman's beliefs about Black women began to change. Today, she is an entirely different person. Not only does she believe that Black women are beautiful, but she knows for certain that we were made in the image of God, and that God didn't make a mistake when He created us. I'm also happy to report that this woman and I are now best friends. We see each other every single day. We have the exact same name. We look identical. We live in the same house, and each morning when I first see her in the mirror, I say "Good morning, Beautiful!"

By now, you may have guessed that *I* was that college student who used to believe that Black women were cursed and viewed as the lowest of women. Throughout this book, you'll learn more about my transformational journey. As you examine your own beliefs and how they affect the way that you view and treat yourself and other Black women, I want you to also realize that you were made in God's image, and that God didn't make a mistake when He created you. As I said in the Introduction, my main goal is for you to accept, appreciate, and love your *inner* and *outer beauty*, and become your best self. So, in this chapter, we'll spend time defining *beauty*, and identifying our beliefs about it. But now, let's begin with the first of many Personal Growth Exercises that I'll ask you to complete.

Personal Growth Exercise: Your Beliefs About Beauty (Part 1)

1.   What is your definition of "beauty?"

_____

_____

_____

_____

_____

_____

2.   Where did your definition of "beauty" come from, and which
individuals and other sources (television, magazines, movies, etc.)
influenced your definition?

_____

_____

_____

_____

_____

_____

3.   Based on your definition of "beauty," do you believe that you are
"beautiful?" Why or why not?

_____

_____

_____

_____

_____

_____

4.   List the names of 3 to 5 women whom you consider to be
"beautiful," and next to each name, explain why each woman fits your
definition of "beauty."

_____

_____

_____

_____

_____

_____

5.   Do your definitions of "beauty" and "beautiful" include both physical appearance (*outer beauty*) and personality, character, behavior, values (*inner beauty*)? Explain your answer.

_____

_____

_____

_____

_____

_____

6.   Based on your definition of "beauty," do you and the women whom you consider to be "beautiful" possess both *inner* and *outer beauty*? Explain your answer.

_____

_____

_____

_____

_____

_____

Beauty and Being Beautiful

Throughout the world, there's a lot of pressure on women to look beautiful. In other words, we're expected to be physically attractive, and often, we're judged--including by other women--by the way that we look. This extreme pressure usually begins in childhood, and it can come from many sources, such as parents or guardians, siblings, other relatives, peers, and the media.

Parents or Guardians

A television program that I watched a few years ago was a perfect example of how parents or guardians can impact the way in which we view ourselves. The show focused on a pregnant Black woman who was carrying twins. When the twins were born, instead of being happy that they were healthy, her first comments were about their appearance. As soon as she saw one twin, she yelled at her husband, "He has a big nose, just like yours! It's your fault." Then, she said that the baby looked "mean." I can only imagine how she would've reacted if the child had been a girl. I also wondered how she would treat this child whom she viewed in such a negative way.

As the previous story illustrates, in some families, the pressure to look beautiful begins at birth. Another example pertains to when I lived in a predominantly Muslim city in northern Cameroon, Africa. During that time, I was surprised to learn that my female neighbors routinely put eye makeup on their infant daughters. I still have pictures of babies and toddlers wearing eye makeup. The next Personal Growth Exercise is related to these examples.

Personal Growth Exercise: Your Beliefs About Beauty (Part 2)

---

1.   Have you ever seen any baby photos of yourself? If so, what do you think about the photo(s)? Do you believe that you were a cute baby, unattractive, etc.? Are you proud of the photo(s)?

_____

_____

_____

_____

_____

_____

2.   What stories have you heard about yourself as a baby and
toddler? Who told them, and how did the stories affect your beliefs
about yourself?

_____

_____

_____

_____

_____

_____

Siblings and Other Relatives

Just as parents and guardians can influence our beliefs about
ourselves, the same is true of our brothers, sisters, and other relatives.
For example, I grew up in the same household with five of my seven
siblings. At an early age, I knew which of the four girls in our house
whom family, friends and acquaintances considered to be *attractive* and
those whom they viewed as *unattractive*. I always knew that I wasn't
one of the pretty ones. So, early on, I grew up believing that most people
were smarter and looked better than I did.

My older sister, who is 11 months older than I am, had a strong
influence on my beliefs about myself. For some reason, this sister always
seemed to hate me. When we were little kids, she bullied me, allowed
others to bully me, and even beat me up on a bus one day. At night, in
the bedroom that we shared, she often reminded me that I was "cursed
by God," and told me that my head was so big that it reminded her of a
horse's head. When my high school senior photos disappeared, and she
later admitted that she had taken them to a local park and burned them,

because she "liked watching my face burn," I was devastated. I cried for days.

Today, I realize that her intense hatred of me, probably stemmed from the fact that we're less than one year apart. Obviously, she may have viewed me as the baby who pushed her out of the way when she was still a baby herself. I'm also happy that throughout the years, our relationship has improved. We chat by telephone, and text each other several times each week.

This sister is also the extended family member whom I am closest to. Now, I try not to get offended when she makes a comment about the size of my head. For example, in 2017, when I texted her a photo of me, she replied, "That's a beautiful picture. Your body has actually caught up to your head, and your head doesn't look big anymore!" Instead of getting my feelings hurt, or becoming self-conscious like I had in the past, I laughed and accepted her comment as a compliment. The next exercise will allow you to examine the impact that your siblings and other relatives have had on your self-image.

Personal Growth Exercise: Your Beliefs About Beauty (Part 3)

1. When you were growing up, what messages did you internalize about your appearance from your siblings and other relatives?

_____

_____

_____

_____

_____

2. How have these messages affected your self-image?

_____

_____

_____

_____

Peers

Our peers can also affect how we feel about ourselves. Two incidents from my childhood are examples. The first occurred at school when I was in sixth grade. The second occurred when I was in high school.

One day, I was excited to wear a new outfit that my mother had bought for me. I was so proud of my green vest, matching skirt, and white blouse that I'm sure I held my head a little higher than usual at school that day. But during lunch time, a popular girl and her group of followers stopped me in my tracks. "Do you own an iron?" she asked. "Yes," I replied, with a confused look on my face. "Then, why don't you use it?" she said, "because your clothes are wrinkled!" Then, she and her followers burst into laughter, and marched off. I was so embarrassed that for the rest of the day, I walked around with my head down, and feeling as small as I usually felt. I couldn't wait to get home and take off that wrinkled outfit.

A similar incident occurred when I was in high school and wore a new outfit to school. Once again, I was pleased with my appearance, and believed that I looked nice. Then, while we were sitting in class, a girl whom I considered to be one of my best friends said, "Your outfit is nice, but you still have a big nose!" I was shocked and embarrassed. Although I'd been told many negative things about myself, no one had ever told me that I had a big nose. Since that day, I've often wondered why a so-called "friend" would make such a statement. Like the sixth-grade bully, I suspect that she wanted to "burst my bubble," and "cut me down to size." Unfortunately, she succeeded. I felt self-conscious for the rest of the day, and developed a negative complex about my nose. Now, I'd like for you to spend time reflecting on and writing about how your peers affected your self-image.

Personal Growth Exercise: Your Beliefs About Beauty (Part 4)

1. When you were growing up, what messages about your appearance did you internalize from friends and other peers?

_____

_____

_____

_____

_____

_____

2. How did these messages affect your beliefs about yourself?

_____

_____

_____

_____

_____

_____

The Media

The media can also affect our views about ourselves. For example, in the United States, television celebrities, and television commercials have made it clear that in order to be beautiful, a woman has to be White: especially a White woman with blond hair and blue eyes.

When I was growing up, I rarely saw Black women on television except in movies, where they were portrayed as slaves, nannies, or housekeepers. But when "Julia," the television show featuring Diahann Carroll, aired, and later, "Good Times," and "The Jeffersons," that changed. In the next section, I'd like for you to explain how television, movies, and other media affected you.

Personal Growth Exercise: Your Beliefs About Beauty (Part 5)

1. When you were growing up, how did television, movies, and other media affect your views about beauty?

_____

_____

_____

_____

_____

_____

2. How did these messages affect your beliefs about yourself?

_____

_____

_____

_____

_____

_____

A Definition of Beauty

Now that I'm a middle-aged woman, my definition of beauty is very different than it was when I was younger. My current definition consists of *inner* and *outer beauty*, but mostly *inner beauty*. However, I'd be lying if I said that *outer beauty* isn't important to me. In fact, each time I look in the mirror and see the fine lines on my forehead or the laugh lines surrounding my mouth, I'm reminded of the fact that I'm growing older. In an attempt to offset the effects of aging, I moisturize my face at least twice each day, and try to exercise daily.

Even though my outward appearance is still very important to me, cultivating *inner beauty* is more important. In Part Two, I'll explain what I mean by *inner beauty*, and why it's more important than *outer beauty*. But in the remaining chapters of Part One, we'll explore several additional topics that are related to *outer beauty*. Next, I introduce a section that I'll end all other chapters with.

Daily Affirmations

Like all human beings, I am a "work in progress." I'm not perfect and never will be. However, I have spent much of my life trying to learn new things that will help me become a better person. In addition to spending time each day reading the Bible, praying, and reading self-help books, I have recently added affirmations to my daily routine. These affirmations consist of "positive self-talk."

The Importance of Positive Self-Talk

Because we are flooded with negative messages about our skin tone, hair texture, body sizes and shapes, physical features, and personalities on a regular basis, it's important for us to be strategic and relentless in drowning out the negative messages, and replacing them with positive messages. Therefore, at the end of each of the remaining chapters, you'll find Daily Affirmations that will help you incorporate positive self-talk into your daily routine, if you aren't already doing so. The more you do this, the more you will begin to believe these positive messages.

My own personal affirmations are positive messages that I tell myself each morning. When I look in the mirror, each morning--before I wash my face, put on makeup, shower, and get dressed--I say "Hello, Beautiful" or "Good morning, Beautiful." This is a strategy that I learned from Cheryl Richardson's *Extreme Self-Care*, a book that I highly recommend. I also have written down a long list of positive messages about myself that I recite each day.

No matter how you currently feel about yourself, I believe that incorporating Daily Affirmations into your regular routine will help you learn to accept, love, treat yourself respectfully, and insist that others treat you respectfully. With this in mind, I'd like for you to read, color, and say each of the following Daily Affirmations at least once each day for the next 21 days. According to some researchers, it takes a minimum of 21 days to break bad habits and develop new ones. Afterwards, color the "Art Therapy" drawings.

I AM BEAUTIFUL.
GOD CREATED ME IN
HIS IMAGE.
I AM NOT A MISTAKE.

Now, create your own Personalized Affirmations to add to this list.

1.

2.

3.

4.

5.

Chapter Two
In the Beginning: Embracing Your Ancestry

Dear Beautiful!

In this chapter, I provide a brief history lesson that is tied to how we as Black women may or may not feel about ourselves. It's impossible for us to discuss our beliefs about beauty without going back to our ancestral roots: Africa. So, before I share my thoughts, please complete the next Personal Growth Exercise.

Personal Growth Exercise: Africa (Part 1)

1. When you were growing up, what did you learn about Africa?

_____

_____

_____

_____

_____

_____

2. Who taught you this information, and how did it affect your self-image, and your views about Africa?

_____

_____

_____

_____

_____

_____

3. List 3 to 5 positive things that you know about Africa.

_____

_____

_____

_____

Africa: Our Ancestral Roots

I hope that it was easy for you to make a list of positive things about Africa. However, if you had trouble doing so, don't feel bad. Most individuals, including Black people, especially in the U.S., have heard a lot of negative stereotypes about Africa, especially from the media. Like most people, until I went to college, I was very ignorant and naïve about Africa. At the University of Southern California, I met African students from Nigeria, Ghana, Kenya, and Zimbabwe. These students taught me a lot of fascinating details about their native countries.

My Trip to Africa

After I graduated from college, I became a Peace Corps Volunteer. This permitted me to live in Africa for nearly two years. As soon as I arrived, I quickly realized how the media and history books have really brainwashed us to view Africa in such a negative way. During that time, I visited Chad, Kenya, Rwanda, and Burundi, and spent 12 weeks in Zaire, (which is now The Democratic Republic of the Congo). But for most of those nearly two years, I lived in Cameroon.

During my time in Africa, I met some wonderful people. I saw many beautiful regions. I ate delicious foods. I spoke Swahili and French. I often wore tailored traditional clothing, and learned about native customs. One of the main questions that I wanted answered was "Where did my ancestors come from?"

So, when people in the Congo told me that I definitely had to be from that region, I was thrilled. I thought I had finally gotten the answer that I needed. However, when I moved to Cameroon, and people told me that I looked like a Cameroonian, I was confused. Therefore, when I returned to the U.S., I still didn't have the answer that I wanted.

In 2017, after taking a DNA test through Ancestry.com, I finally got the answer. The results revealed that I am 92% African! The biggest percentage of my African ancestry (26%), is actually from Cameroon and the Congo. This means that long ago, the Africans who told me that I had to have come from those regions, were actually correct! The second largest percentage of my African ancestry (21%) is from the Ivory Coast and Ghana; 17% is Nigerian, 10% is from Benin and Togo, 7% is from Mali, and 6% is from Senegal.

Learning about my African ancestry empowered me. It also cleared up stories that I'd heard about the "Indian blood" in our family. The DNA test revealed that my ancestry is *only* 1% Native American. Furthermore, even though I had been told that we don't have "any White blood" in us, the test revealed that my ancestry is 6% European.

Personal Growth Exercise: Africa (Part 2)

1. Now, that you've read about my experiences in Africa, how has your opinion of Africa changed, if at all?

_____

_____

_____

_____

_____

_____

2. What questions do you have about Africa?

_____

_____

_____

_____

_____

_____

Ten Facts About Africa

Here are some facts about Africa from the World Atlas online.

1. Africa is the "birthplace of mankind."
2. Africa is a continent, not a country.
3. There are "54 countries" in Africa.
4. "Africa is the second most populous continent, after Asia."
5. More than "one billion" people live in Africa.
6. More than "a thousand languages are spoken in Africa," and "Africa is the most multilingual continent in the world."
7. There were many ancient kingdoms in Africa, including in Ghana, Mali, and Benin.
8. Africa's Nile River is "considered to be the largest river in the world."
9. Africa's Sahara Desert is "the world's hottest desert."
10. Nelson Mandela was one of the most famous African leaders in recent times.

You can learn more about Africa, your ancestry, and Black history by reading the following books and visiting the following websites:

Books

- *The Gift of Black Folks: The Negroes in the Making of America* by Dr. W.E.B. DuBois
- *The Negro in the Making of America* by Benjamin Quarles
- *A School History of the Negro Race in America From 1619 to 1890: With a Short Introduction as to the Origin of the Race: Also a Short Sketch of Liberia* by Edward A. Johnson
- *In Their Own Words: A History of the American Negro 1865-1916* by Milton Meltzer
- *Prince Among Slaves* by Terry Alford

Websites

- Blackpast.org.

- Association for the Study of African American Life and History: https://asalh.org/
- Smithsonian National Museum of African American History & Culture: https://nmaahc.si.edu/
- World Atlas: http://www.worldatlas.com/webimage/countrys/af.htm.

Personal Growth Exercise: Africa (Part 3)

---

1. List at least 3 things that you are willing to do in order to increase your knowledge about Africa. For example, you might decide to trace your roots, read books about Africa, Google "Africa," take a "virtual" trip to Africa by watching videos on the internet, visit an African restaurant, etc.

_____

_____

_____

_____

_____

_____

I AM BEAUTIFUL.

GOD CREATED ME IN HIS IMAGE.

AFRICA IS AN AMAZING CONTINENT.

MY ANCESTORS CAME FROM AFRICA.

I AM PROUD OF MY AFRICAN ANCESTRY.

Now, please look at the map of Africa below, and:

- Color the map and draw images or write words that reflect your views about Africa.

- For example, you might draw diamonds, gold, animals, trees, plants, or people whom you think might resemble your ancestors, or write the names of various African countries where your ancestors may have lived, or the names of various African languages.

- Whatever you do with the map, please make it as beautiful as you are.

Chapter Three
Learning to Love and Accept Your Skin Tone

Dear Beautiful!

I recently heard an attractive Black woman make several negative remarks about her skin tone and weight. Her comments saddened me for two reasons: First, although she is the mother of an adult daughter and son, she is still being very self-critical, and failing to recognize her own God-given *outer beauty*. Second, she reminded me of how I use to be: the college student who believed that dark-skinned Black women were cursed.

Unfortunately, this woman isn't alone, for what she believes about herself is common among women throughout the world. This is why bleaching creams and skin lighteners continue to be popular. Recently, a Filipina told me that she grew up believing that she was unattractive because of her "dark" skin tone. When I lived in Africa, my Cameroonian seamstress often bleached her skin. Many Asian American women carry umbrellas on sunny days in order to prevent their skin from darkening.

On the other hand, some women have been taught to dislike their light skin tone. For this reason, many White women spend money at tanning booths, lay in the sunlight for hours, and risk getting skin cancer in order to darken their skin. In fact, just as the skin lightening industry is popular, the same is true of the skin darkening industry!

A recent case illustrates the degree to which some White women harbor self-hatred: In 2015, the news media revealed that Rachel Dolezal, a NAACP leader, was actually a woman who was born "White." However, she had darkened her skin, changed her hair texture, and pretended to be a Black woman for years. So, in this chapter, we'll focus on another aspect of *outer beauty*: skin tone. Let's start with another Personal Growth Exercise.

Personal Growth Exercise: Your Skin (Part 1)

1. How would you describe your skin tone?

_____

_____

_____

_____

_____

_____

2. How do you feel about your skin tone, and why do you feel this way?

_____

_____

_____

_____

_____

_____

3. What have other people told you about your skin tone, and how have those messages affected you?

_____

_____

_____

_____

_____

_____

Key Points About Skin Tone

In *A Brighter Day: How Parents Can Help African American Youth*, I wrote extensively about "skin tone." In that book, I described the "Color Caste System" that has caused many Black women to believe that beauty can only be found in light skin, and that dark skin is ugly. I also described a dark-skinned woman who had mistreated her light-skinned daughter out of jealousy. Here's a summary of some of the key points that I made in that chapter of *A Brighter Day*:

- "In order to have healthy self-esteem as adults, and in order to help our children develop healthy self-esteem, we must deal with" our issues about skin tone.
- "We must accept our skin tone as not being inferior or superior to anyone else's."
- "We must accept our children's skin tone no matter how light, dark, or different it may look from our own."
- "From the moment that a child is born, we must begin to build that child up, instead of rejecting him or her because the child is 'too dark' or 'too light,' etc."
- "We should never show favoritism among our children, especially because of the children's skin tone."[1]

Personal Growth Exercise: Your Skin (Part 2)

1. How do you treat and view Black women whose skin tone is lighter than your own, and why?

_____

_____

_____

_____

_____

_____

2. How do you treat and view Black women whose skin tone is darker than your own, and why?

_____

_____

_____

_____

3. Do you feel superior or inferior to women whose skin tones are lighter or darker than your own? Why or why not?

_____

_____

_____

_____

_____

Accepting and Loving Our God-Given Skin Tone

One of my favorite activities is watching the sunset at our local beach. During this time, I thank God for His many blessings, and often sing or hum songs of praise. During the year that I've been sunset watching, I've learned an important fact: No two sunsets are identical! Sometimes, clouds hide all or part of the sun as it is setting. Sometimes, the sun looks like a huge orange ball. Sometimes, the sky surrounding the setting sun looks pink, grey, pale blue, lavender, or some other color. No matter how many sunsets I watch, I always see something new.

On several rare occasions, I've been blessed to witness the "Green Flash." Bestselling author Victor Villasenor told me about the "Green Flash," when I saw him at the beach one evening. Occasionally, on days when there are no low clouds blocking the sun, right before the sun totally disappears from view, a green flash will appear. Since Victor told me about it, I've seen the "Green Flash" about eight times. Each time, I've marveled at the beauty that God put on this earth for us to enjoy. I'm also amazed at the uniqueness of each sunset and the different colors that appear.

These colors, as well as the colors of flowers, plants, birds, butterflies, the ocean, and animals, remind me of a fact that I'll keep repeating throughout this book:

God likes, color, diversity, and uniqueness. If He had wanted us all to have the same hair texture, features, body sizes, shapes, personalities, and skin tone, He would've created us to look and act in identical ways.

Shortly after I wrote this statement, I heard Joel Osteen, a pastor and motivational speaker whom I watch daily on television, make a similar statement about the importance of accepting our uniqueness. The next Personal Growth Exercise is related to this quote.

Personal Growth Exercise: Your Skin (Part 3)

---

1. Explain why you agree or disagree with the statement "**God likes color, diversity, and uniqueness. If He had wanted us all to have the same hair texture, features, body sizes, shapes, personalities, and skin tone, He would've created us to look and act in identical ways,**" and explain the reasons why you agree or disagree.

_____

_____

_____

_____

_____

_____

Why This Quote is So Important

There's an important reason why I asked you to think and write about the quote, and why I'll keep repeating it throughout this book: As I've previously stated--from childhood onward, Black women are assaulted with negative messages about their appearance, personalities, behavior, and worth--on an ongoing basis. So, in order to drown out the negative messages that are designed to minimize us, make us feel stupid, ugly, worthless, and keep us from reaching our God-ordained destinies, I'll keep repeating this point. Just as I'll keep sharing it with *you*, I also have to remind *myself* of this quote on a regular basis. Here's a related personal story.

"Too Dark-Skinned to Wear Red?"

In March 2017, I was invited to give a keynote address and a conference presentation in two different California cities during the same week. Whenever I have speaking engagements, I spend a lot of time praying about what to say, preparing the actual presentation, practicing the presentation, and selecting the best outfit to wear. I do these things because being well prepared, and looking my very best increase my confidence level.

During that week in March, as I prepared for the speaking engagements, deciding what to wear to the keynote address wasn't a problem for me. Since it would take place in northern California, I knew that I could wear a periwinkle-colored suit-- a matching jacket and skirt set-- that I'd recently worn to another presentation. The second presentation, however, would take place in San Diego, my childhood hometown, which is about an hour's drive from my current home. This meant that some of the conference attendees may have attended one of the other recent presentations that I'd given in southern California.

Because I didn't want to wear an outfit that the San Diego conference attendees may have already seen me wearing, my clothing options were limited. When I narrowed them down to finding (1) something that I could fit into at the time, (2) something that was appropriate for the weather, and (3) something that I hadn't worn recently to a presentation, only one option remained: a bright red suit that consisted of a matching jacket and skirt.

Since red is one of my least favorite colors, I wasn't happy with this option. I've never felt that I look attractive in this color, unless it was a dark or wine-colored red. Part of the reason was that a negative message I'd internalized since childhood was buried in my self-conscious: "You're too dark-skinned to wear bright colors, especially red." So, in my desperate search for something else to wear, I even went shopping the day before the San Diego presentation. But no matter how many stores I visited, I couldn't find another option that I liked.

On the day of the presentation, before getting dressed, I searched my closet once again for another outfit. In the end, I was stuck with the red suit. After I put it on, in order to "spice up," my appearance, I added large silver hoop earrings, a red and silver necklace, and silver bracelets. Then, I took a selfie on my cellphone, and headed to the conference site: a San Diego hotel.

As soon as I got out of my car, a Black woman in the hotel parking lot said, "I like that red suit!" A few minutes later, another woman complimented me. Their comments made me feel a lot better about the suit. Later that day, when I looked at the selfie, I'd taken earlier, I saw that I looked better than I could've imagined, and even liked the photo: red suit and all.

The strangest aspect of my hang up about wearing red clothing is that I actually love bright colors, especially pastels. I love blue, pink, purple, and other pastels, but fuchsia, is one of my favorites. When I wear fuchsia clothing and nail polish, I feel better, feel more attractive, and feel more confident. The world looks brighter and there's more pep in my step. Wearing pale pink clothing and nail polish also has a positive effect on me. In the next exercise, I'd like for you to describe your beliefs about "colors."

Personal Growth Exercise: Your Skin (Part 4)

1. What are your favorite colors, and why do you like them?

_____

_____

_____

_____

_____

_____

2. Which colors do you wear that get you the most compliments from others?

_____

_____

_____

_____

_____

_____

3. Which colors do you enjoy wearing and believe you look best in, and why?

_____

_____

_____

_____

_____

_____

4. Which colors do you hate to wear, and why?

_____

_____

_____

_____

_____

_____

5. Are there any colors that you believe you are "too dark" or "too light skinned" to wear? If so, where did these beliefs come from?

_____

_____

_____

_____

_____

6. Now, examine all of your answers, and write a sentence or two, explaining what you can learn from them.

_____

_____

_____

_____

_____

_____

Accepting and Valuing the God-Given Skin Tone of *Others*

Whenever someone asks my friend Wanda, what "color" a Black baby is, she always gives the same answer: "A baby color." It doesn't matter if the baby is dark skinned, light skinned, or in-between those skin tone ranges. Wanda's answer is the same: "a baby color." Her point is that all babies are beautiful regardless of their skin tone, and only a petty, small-minded person will judge a baby's beauty based on his/her skin tone. Yet, because of their own unaddressed issues about skin tone, adults-- including some Black women-- often do this.

So, as Black women, part of our journey to loving and accepting our *inner* and *outer beauty* requires that we learn to be as open-minded and as positive about the skin tone of Black babies and adults as my friend Wanda is. If you aren't already doing so, I hope that you'll become strategic and deliberate in not only accepting but valuing the skin tone of other Black folks: both adults and children. After all, just as God gave you the skin tone that He wanted you to have, He also did the same for others, even if their skin tone is very different from yours. One of the ways that we can learn to accept and value the skin tone of other Black women is to compliment them. The next Personal Growth Exercise is related to this point.

Personal Growth Exercise: Your Skin (Part 5)

1. How often do you receive compliments from other women, how do you respond, and why?

_____

_____

_____

_____

_____

_____

2. What are some specific compliments that you have received from other women, and how did you respond, and feel about the compliments?

_____

_____

_____

_____

_____

_____

3. How often do you give compliments to other women, and why?

_____

_____

_____

_____

_____

4. Which types of women are you more likely to compliment, and why?

_____

_____

_____

_____

_____

5. What are some specific compliments that you give to other women?

_____

_____

_____

_____

_____

_____

6. Now, review your previous answers, and explain what you learned from them.

_____

_____

_____

_____

_____

_____

Knowing What Your Skin Needs

The process of learning to love and accept our skin tone includes learning as much as possible about our skin, what it needs, and how to care for it. In other words, TLC--Tender, Love, and Care--is vital for our skin. For example, when I was younger, my skin was very oily, and didn't need a lot of moisture. The makeup that I used needed to be oil free. As I've grown older, however, my skin has lost a lot of its natural oil. Therefore, I've learned the importance of moisturizing it in the morning and at night. But one of the most important things that I've learned about my skin and body is that I am very allergic to many foods, animals, plants, and chemicals. So, I have to make sure that the products that I use don't create an allergic reaction for me. In the last Personal Growth Exercise of this chapter, I'd like for you to explain what you know about your skin, and describe your TLC Plan for it.

Personal Growth Exercise: Your Skin (Part 6)

1. What does your skin need in order to be healthy?

    _____

    _____

    _____

    _____

    _____

    _____

2. Which products and practices are good for your skin, and why?

    _____

    _____

    _____

    _____

    _____

    _____

3. Which products and practices are harmful to your skin, and why?

    _____

    _____

    _____

    _____

    _____

    _____

4. How do you show love and appreciation for your skin each day?
    What new healthy routines are you willing to add?

    _____

    _____

    _____

    _____

I AM BEAUTIFUL.
GOD CREATED ME IN
HIS IMAGE.
MY SKIN TONE IS
BEAUTIFUL.
I LOVE MY SKIN.
I AM PROUD OF MY
AMAZING AFRICAN
ANCESTRY.

Art Therapy

Directions: Under each of the following words, draw something or write a word that describes your feelings about it. For example, under the word "red," you might draw and color a red apple or a happy face, or you might write, "love it" or "hate it," depending on how you feel about the color red.

red	blue	yellow	green	white
pink	purple	fuchsia	orange	cream
burgundy	off white	periwinkle	mauve	black
beige	turquoise	lime	plum	lavender
peach	gray	gold	silver	bronze
violet	lilac	plum	emerald	lemon
ivory	indigo	khaki	magenta	maroon

On the following page, look at each face. Add the features, and hair textures that you would like to create. Color each face in a different shade, ranging from very dark to medium, and very light. Under each face write the words "You are beautiful."

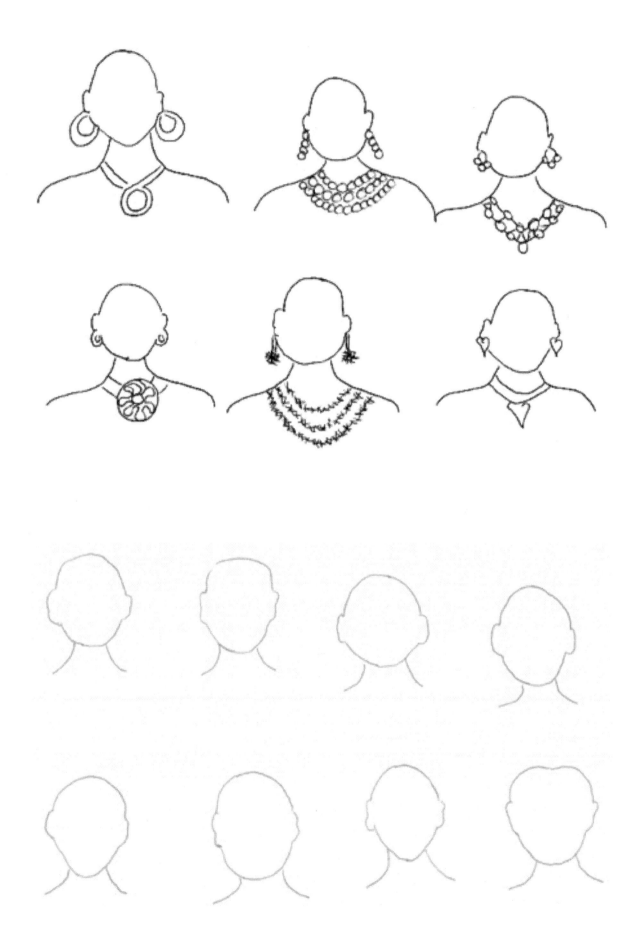

Chapter Four

Learning to Love and Accept Your Hair

Dear Beautiful!

Like skin tone, hair texture has always been a great source of pride or pain for many Black women. During childhood, some of us were told by parents, guardians, or other individuals that we had "good hair," "nappy hair," or "bad hair." *Good hair*, of course, resembled hair texture that was naturally straight, possibly somewhat wavy, and very similar to the hair texture of White folks. Hair texture consisting of naturally tight curls was considered to be *bad, nappy, or kinky*, and a lot of us suffered burned ears, scalps and necks from straightening combs or chemicals designed to "relax" or "tame" our hair.

Comedian Chris Rock made a movie about our hair issues. Author Bell Hooks wrote a children's book titled *Happy to Be Nappy*, and a White teacher had to run for her life, after teaching the book *Nappy Hair* to her fifth graders. So, in this chapter, my goal is to help you identify and address any hair issues that you have, and most important: to encourage you to learn to love and accept your hair texture, no matter what it is. The following Personal Growth Exercise is a starting point.

Personal Growth Exercise: Your Hair (Part 1)

---

1. How would you describe your hair texture?

_____

_____

_____

_____

_____

2. How do you feel about your hair texture, and why?

_____

_____

3.   During childhood, what messages did you hear about your hair texture, from whom did you hear them, and how were you affected?

_____

_____

_____

_____

_____

_____

A Recent Personal "Hair" Story

In October 2017, for the first time in more than 30 years, I wore my hair in an Afro in public. When my husband, Rufus, saw me, he said "You look marvelous," grabbed his cellphone, and began taking photos of me. He also told me that I looked much younger wearing the Afro than the combination ponytail/Afro Puff that I usually wore. After seeing a text of me in my Afro, my eldest sister, Tracy, who had already been wearing an Afro, texted "that looks good," and included emojis of a heart and a happy face. During "Face Time," my daughter, NaChe', said my hair looked great. When I texted my "Afro Selfie" to a White female coworker of mine, she wrote, "Ohhh, I love it!!!" Another White female coworker texted, "I love it!!!," and my friend Dr. Jenny Rankin, who happens to be White, texted, "Ohhh, BEAUTIFUL!" A few minutes later, she showed my "Afro Selfie" to her husband, Lane. Lane is my husband's close friend and the founder and former CEO of the company at which my Rufus and I work. Dr. Jenny texted me: "Lane agreed you look beautiful."

Although I really appreciated every compliment, I also informed Rufus, NaChe', coworkers, sister, and Dr. Jenny that I would only be wearing my Afro for *one day*, while travelling to Central California for a speaking engagement. I also informed them that the next day--as usual-- I would use gel to smooth my hair into the ponytail/Afro Puff that I'd been wearing for the past two years since I first stopped using chemical relaxers on my hair. Before I finish this story, I'd like for you to complete a related Personal Growth Exercise.

| Personal Growth Exercise: Your Hair (Part 2) |

1.   Which hairstyles do you prefer to wear, and why?

_____

_____

_____

_____

_____

_____

2.   Which hairstyles do you dislike wearing, and why?

_____

_____

_____

_____

_____

_____

3.   Have you ever worn your hair in an Afro, Afro Puff, or braids in public, especially to work or school? Why or why not?

_____

_____

_____

_____

_____

_____

4. In your opinion, why did I wear my Afro in public one day, but not the following day for my work-related presentation?

_____

_____

_____

_____

_____

_____

The Story Behind the Story

I loved the way that my Afro looked and felt, and all of the related compliments. I also loved the fact that styling my hair in an Afro took a lot less time than using gel to create the ponytail/Afro Puff hairstyle. In spite of this, there were several reasons why I didn't wear my Afro during my Professional Development workshop for school leaders.

The first reason was that I wanted my Afro to be larger when I started wearing it in public on a regular basis. The second reason was that I needed more time to get used to seeing myself wearing an Afro, rather than the ponytail/Afro Puff that I'd grown used to wearing. But a more pressing reason was that "Since my work focuses on "Equity," especially helping educators work more effectively with African American, Latino, and low-income students, I didn't want anyone in the audience to use his or her stereotypes about women wearing Afros, as an excuse to ignore my message.

Stereotypes About Our Hair and Hairstyles

My concern about the audience's potential negative reaction to my Afro was legitimate. Just as Black folks are bombarded with stereotypes about every aspect of our being from childhood onward, the same is true of our hairstyles and hair texture. For example, in a 2017 National Public Radio article, Kayla Lattimore revealed the following:

In recent years, Black girls have been sent home for wearing dreads, head wraps, and even wearing their hair naturally. In schools across the country, Black student suspension rates are higher than their peers.' In charter schools, kindergarten through eighth grade, those rates are even higher.[1]

Having to deal with stereotypes is tough for adults, but even sadder for children, especially when they are punished as a result of someone else's fear, stereotypes, and ignorance.

As a highly-educated professional woman, I personally have been subjected to stereotypes and blatant racism from teachers and school leaders during some of my Professional Development workshops. For example, in West Palm Beach, Florida, one teacher stormed out of the room during the first 15 minutes of my presentation. At this same school, the principal, who happened to be a White woman, snatched the microphone out of my hands *twice* and demanded that I "say what we are paying you to say!" Despite her unprofessionalism and efforts to control and silence me, I continued to say what needed to be said: the truth about how educators can work more effectively with African American, Latino, and low-income students. In California, an educator called me the "N word," before I even began my presentation. In Texas, South Carolina, and California, some educators have been so rude and resistant to my presentations that I've had to ask them to leave, so that others who may have wanted to listen, could hear what I had to say.

Are Some Folks Scared of Our Hair?

Previously, I mentioned that several individuals, including my sister, Tracy, gave me compliments about my Afro. Although I shared part of her text-- "That looks good"-- I didn't share the second part of her text: "You know White people get scared of Fros." And apparently, she was correct!

When I Googled, "Are White people afraid of Afros?" numerous articles surfaced. The first was titled "13 Crazy Things White People

Think About Black Natural Hair at Work and School." The 13 stereotypes included the beliefs that Afros and natural hairstyles are dirty, unprofessional, and signs of rebellion and militancy. The article also revealed that despite the fact that negative stereotypes about Afros and natural hairstyles are common, Whites often ask if they can touch Afros.[2] This last statement reminded me of a similar experience that I had when I wore an Afro during my college years.

One summer, I worked as an Intern Reporter for a newspaper in Oregon. One of my coworkers, an experienced reporter, asked if she could touch my hair and the hair of my roommate. My roommate, who was also an Intern Reporter, happened to be a biracial (half-Black and half-White) female college student. We were in the busiest and most populated room of the building, when the reporter put one hand on my head and the other on the head of my roommate. Then, she said loudly, "It feels just like brillo!" At that moment, I felt as if every other employee was staring at me, and I wanted to disappear.

Although the woman's comment and lie offended and embarrassed me, I can't remember if I responded verbally or not. But I've never forgotten that blatant example of workplace cultural insensitivity. The next Personal Growth Exercise can help you uncover any negative beliefs that you have about Afros, Afro Puffs, braids, and other natural hairstyles for Black women.

Personal Growth Exercise: Your Hair (Part 3)

---

1.   Have you ever been judged, stereotyped, disrespected, teased, or bullied as a result of your hair texture or hairstyle? If so, who were the perpetrators, and how were you affected?

_____

_____

_____

_____

_____

_____

2.   Have *you* ever judged, stereotyped, disrespected, teased, or bullied another woman as a result of her hair texture or hairstyle? If so, who was the victim, how did she react, and why did you do what you did?

_____

_____

_____

_____

_____

_____

Getting Real and Moving Forward

In order to learn to accept and love our God-given hair texture, we must know what's good and bad for our hair by educating ourselves. For example, my scalp used to start itching after beauticians would color it with over-the-counter popular hair colors, and I never could understand why. It took a traumatic experience for me to learn what the itching meant: I am allergic to traditional hair coloring products. As a result of my ignorance and failure to listen to the message that my scalp was sending me, I ended up having a huge allergic reaction that made my hair fall out. I had to wear a wig for an entire year until it grew back.

During that year, my daughter, Dr. Nafissa Thompson-Spires, told me about HennaforHair.Com, which not only contains a wealth of information about hair care and hair coloring, but the website also sells plant-based hair-coloring products that I can use. Furthermore, Nafissa and my daughter, NaChe,' shared many important hair-care tips, and video links with me that helped me transition from using relaxers to learning how to grow and take care of my own hair. This has been an empowering experience and now I fully understand what my hair needs: moisture, the use-of wide-tooth combs, protective hairstyles at bedtime, limited or no heat, and satin-lined sleep caps that don't put pressure on my edges. I've also enjoyed watching some of the wonderful videos that Black women have created to educate others. Lately, I've been learning how to create "Twists Outs," as a result of these videos, and I'm very excited about wearing my hair this way!

An Update

About a month after I wrote most of this chapter, I celebrated a milestone birthday. This birthday was a huge blessing to me for many reasons. The most important was that it reminded me that God has blessed me to live *at least 20 years longer* than my father and three of my younger siblings lived. This birthday also brought out my natural inner boldness. Instead of caring about the opinions of others, I decided to wear my Afro to my current job in Corporate America for the first time.

Contrary to what I expected, many of my coworkers told me that they loved my hair. In fact, that day, I received more compliments than I ever have on any other day. This experience taught me that even though a lot of people may have stereotypes about our hair, not everyone is that way. Therefore, we shouldn't make assumptions about how people will react.

Since then, I've worn my Afro to work every day. Wearing it has empowered me. I love how I look and feel, which is more beautiful, more confident, and more authentic. The final Personal Growth Exercise in this chapter, and the Art Therapy, and Daily Affirmations will move you closer to learning to love, appreciate, learn what's best, and accept your God-given hair texture.

Personal Growth Exercise: Your Hair (Part 4)

---

1.   Which products are harmful to your hair, and why?

_____

_____

_____

_____

_____

_____

2.   Which products are good for your hair, and why?

_____

_____

_____

_____

_____

3.   Which styles are good for your hair, and why?

_____

_____

_____

_____

_____

4.   Which hair routines and practices are good for your hair, and why?

_____

_____

_____

_____

_____

5.   What steps are you willing to take in order to show love and appreciation for your God-given natural hair texture?

_____

_____

_____

_____

_____

6.   Review your previous answers, and use what you learn from them

to create your "I-Love-My-Hair Action Plan."

_____

_____

_____

_____

_____

_____

I AM BEAUTIFUL.
GOD CREATED ME IN
HIS IMAGE.
I LOVE MY SKIN TONE,
AFRICAN ANCESTRY,
AND BEAUTIFUL
HAIR TEXTURE.

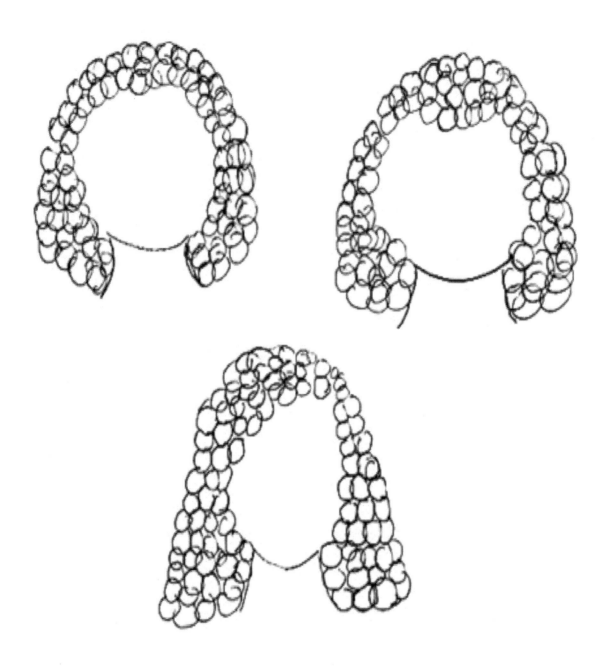

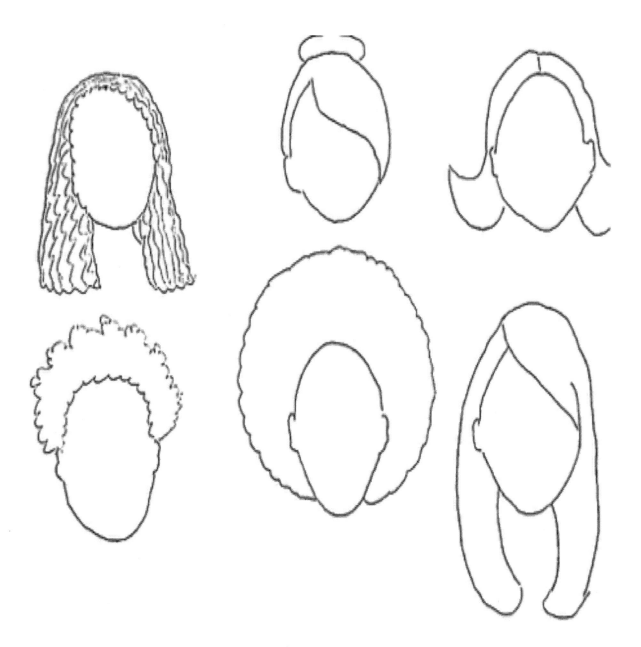

Chapter Five

Learning to Love, Respect and Accept Your Body

Dear Beautiful!

One evening in September 2017, as I was strolling along the pier at my favorite southern California beach, I heard an interesting remark from a stranger: "I'm *good* looking!" the man declared to the woman with whom he was walking. As I continued to stroll, I kept thinking about his bold comment. I knew that I'd *heard* him correctly, but wanted to make sure that I'd *seen* him correctly. So, even though it was night time, I put on my sunglasses, turned around, and headed back to where the couple stood. When I approached them, the sunglasses allowed me to get a good look at him without appearing to be staring.

Sure enough, I had *seen* him correctly. He was about my height-- 5 feet 4 inches tall-- had a grey crew cut, a receding hairline, and tanned skin. He also appeared to be in the 65-to-70-year-old age range. In spite of this, the man not only *believed* that he was attractive, but was audacious enough to say it loudly. His middle-aged companion heard him and so did I. In the following Personal Growth Exercise, please share your thoughts about this story.

Personal Growth Exercise: Your Body (Part 1)

---

1.   Are you as confident about your physical appearance as this man was? Why or why not?

_____

_____

_____

_____

_____

_____

2.   In your opinion, what are the differences between bragging, being conceited, and being self-confident?

_____

_____

_____

_____

_____

_____

A Double Whammy: Body Image and Body Shaming

I shared the previous story with you, because it relates to another aspect of *outer beauty*: body image. As Black women, just as we've been overwhelmed by negative messages about our value, skin tones, hair texture, and ancestry, we've also received negative messages about our body shapes and sizes. Therefore, I can realistically assume that most of us aren't as confident about our *outer* appearance as the man in the previous story. We also get a double-whammy: body shaming from Black folks, as well as from non-Blacks.

The first "whammy" or source of shaming may come from other Black people. For example, some Black males make it clear that they find "big booties" attractive, and someone even sang a song about "Baby Got Back." I suspect that the song is praising "Baby" for having a big rear end. On the other hand, Black females who have smaller rear ends, may be teased by other Blacks for not having "enough back."

The second "whammy" or source of shaming may come from non-Blacks. Even though some Black folks equate big rear ends with beauty, and medical butt enhancements, have become popular, many non-Blacks don't view large butts as attractive. For this reason, Black girls who attend predominantly White schools have often been teased and shamed by their non-Black peers for having big butts. One of the worse cases that I know involved adult body shamers.

Many years ago, after I conducted a Professional Development workshop in West Palm Beach, Florida, a Black teacher told me two stories that upset me. The first story pertained to a Black sixth-grade boy. This student was arrested for leaving the cafeteria without permission in order to use the school restroom. The second story involved Black girls at the school. These students were receiving low grades in their dance class from White female teachers who told them that because of their body shapes, they couldn't get into the correct ballet poses. In other words, these girls were being penalized for something that they couldn't control: the natural shapes of their bodies. Before reading a very famous story about body shaming, please complete the next Personal Growth Exercise.

Personal Growth Exercise: Your Body (Part 2)

1.   How do you feel about your body?

_____
_____
_____
_____
_____
_____

2.   How do you treat your body?

_____
_____
_____
_____
_____
_____

3.   What messages have you heard from others about your body, and how did the messages affect you?

_____
_____
_____

_____

_____

_____

4.   If you could do *one thing* to change your body, what would it be, and why?

_____

_____

_____

_____

_____

5.   When you're in the presence of women who are thinner than you are, how do you feel and behave? What are your reasons for feeling and behaving as you do?

_____

_____

_____

_____

_____

6.   When you're in the presence of women who are heavier than you are, how do you feel and behave? What are your reasons for feeling and behaving as you do?

_____

_____

_____

_____

Now, let me share another "body shaming" story with you. It's one of the worse and most infamous stories that I know about the historic shaming of Black female bodies. **Warning: This story is very sad, so feel free to skip it, and go to the next section, after Personal Growth Exercise 3 if you'd like.**

The Tragic Case of Sara "Saartjie" Baartman

Sara Baartman (the name that was given to her by her Dutch owner) was born in South Africa in 1789. Her short life was painful, to say the least. When Sara was two years old, her mother died. Several years later, when her father, a "cattle driver" died, she became an orphan. Sara was still very young when she married a drummer. By the time that she was 16 years old, both her husband-- who was murdered by Whites-- and her newborn baby were dead.[1]

At some point, Sara allegedly developed a "medical condition" that made her life even worse. According to a recent BBC Magazine article, Sara's condition was called "steatopygia." However, although the Internet contains a lot of information about "steatopygia" and its racist origins, credible online medical sources, such as webmd.com and mayoclinic.org-- two resources that I often use-- contain no references to it. Sara's so-called "steatopygia" allegedly caused her to have "extremely protuberant buttocks due to a build-up of fat."[2] The large size, shape and coloring of her rear end led to her being exploited for money.

When Sara was 20 or 21 years old, a White doctor took her from South Africa to London by ship. In London, Sara was treated like a freak, put into circuses, and paraded around nearly naked, publicly and in private homes, so that Europeans could pay money to see and touch her body.[3] Four years later, Sara was taken to Paris, sold to another man, and placed in a cage with a "baby rhinoceros." According to one article:

> Her "trainer" would order her to sit or stand in a similar way that circus animals are ordered. At times Baartman was displayed almost completely naked, wearing little more than a tan loincloth, and she was only allowed that, due to her insistence that she cover what was culturally sacred. She was nicknamed "Hottentot Venus."[4]

Sara died at age 26, and the cause of her death is unknown. Some believed that it was pneumonia, smallpox, or alcoholism. But after her death, the disrespect continued. Her body was dissected, and put into jars. The jars were displayed in a museum, so that people could continue to view her as a "freak." In 1981, after Stephen Jay Gould wrote about her in *The Mismeasure of Man*, her story finally received the attention and public outrage that it deserved. South African President Nelson Mandela requested that the French government return Sara's remains to her homeland. Thanks to President Mandela, nearly 200 years after her death, Sara's remains were given a proper burial.[5]

Sharing Sara's story with you was a very painful ordeal for me, and each time that I read it, tears form in my eyes. I know that reading this story may have also stirred up a lot of emotions within you. The story is also a reminder that every day, throughout the world, children and women from all racial backgrounds are exploited by sexual deviants and perverts. The "Sex Trafficking Industry" is just one example of this, but rape and child molestation are also common problems. The next Personal Growth Exercise will allow you to vent and share your reactions and thoughts about Sara's story.

Personal Growth Exercise: Your Body (Part 3)

---

1. What do you think of Sara's story?

_____

_____

_____

_____

_____

_____

2. How did you feel as you were reading it?

_____

_____

_____

_____

3.   What lessons did this story teach you about history, body shaming, exploitation, and other related topics?

_____

_____

_____

_____

_____

_____

My Struggle to Accept My Body

I'm very thankful to God that my life and experiences haven't been like Sara Baartman's. Nevertheless, like many women, especially Black women in the U.S., for most of my life, I've struggled to accept my body. As a college freshman, when I weighed 110 pounds, I was obsessed with my "huge gut." After giving birth to my first child, I believed that I was "fat" for weighing 150 pounds. During my third pregnancy, when I weighed 215 pounds, I was extremely depressed, and became too embarrassed to even go to my own mailbox during daytime. Many years later, after I'd lost more than 100 pounds, when a friend said "Gail, I didn't know you have big hips," I felt insulted.

My struggle to accept my body image, size, and shape (which used to be "hourglass shaped," but has become more "pear shaped" as I age), has caused me to constantly think that I was too fat, and that my hips, abdomen, and butt were too big. As a result, I've been on way too many diets and exercise programs. Some of these practices did more harm than good. For example, when I was in high school and college, in an effort to have a flatter "stomach," I use to do *at least* 100 sit-ups every night. When I was a high school teacher, I use to do "step aerobics" every night. Today, I believe that my knee problems, backaches, and arthritis, may be related to these unhealthy practices.

I currently work for a company at which there's only one other Black female, and I'm one of the oldest women. This means that the majority of my female coworkers are much younger than I am. Some are also much thinner. Each time that I see a younger, thinner coworker, I literally have to "kill" negative thoughts in my head, such as "You're fat. You're old. You have a huge stomach. You have a big butt!" One of the ways that I combat these negative thoughts is to make an effort to focus on *myself* and remember that:

I'm unique. I'm special. I'm God's child. Although I'm not perfect and never will be, I'm fine, just as I am at this moment and stage of my life, for I am one of God's beautiful creations, and He didn't make a mistake when He created me.

It took me a long time to get to this point in life-- to gain this perspective-- and it's still a daily struggle. So, in the remainder of this chapter, we'll focus on the importance of loving and respecting *your* body, and explore several related topics. By the time that you get to the end of this chapter, even if you aren't able to be as bold as the middle-aged man in knee-length shorts on the pier was, I want you to remember his story, and become as self-accepting and confident as he was.

Knowing What's Best for Your Body

Your body is very important, because how you treat it may determine how long you'll live, and the quality of life that you'll have as you grow older. Researchers and doctors have found that numerous diseases and health problems are caused by what we eat and how we treat our bodies. Sometimes, the consequences of our choices early in life and how we treated our bodies, don't show up until much later. So, no matter how old you are today, it's important to make sure that you're making healthy decisions.

This means that the journey to loving and accepting your God-given body includes knowing what's good for your body, what's bad for it, and learning to treat it respectfully. These are lessons that I've repeatedly had to learn the hard way. For example, I've damaged my feet by wearing shoes that were too tight, and standing in high heels for too long. Years ago, I wore a pair of ankle-length boots on a flight from California to Canada. During the trip, my feet swelled so badly, that by the time I reached my hotel in Montreal, I was hobbling. As a result of that incident, I have a daily remember of the importance of treating my feet respectfully: a huge bunion on my right foot!

In addition to learning how to take better care of my feet by giving myself homemade pedicures, making sure that my shoes are wide enough, and that the heels are appropriate for the amount of walking and standing that I need to do, I have spent many years learning about healthy living, and what my body needs. Before I share more of what I've learned, I'd like for you to complete the next Personal Growth Exercise.

Personal Growth Exercise: Your Body (Part 4)

1.   How well do you know and understand your body?

_____

_____

_____

_____

_____

_____

2.   What types of shoes and shoe sizes are best for you?

_____

_____

_____

_____

_____

_____

3.	How much sleep does your body need, and what is the average amount of sleep that you get each night?

_____

_____

_____

_____

_____

_____

4.	What types of foods are best for your body, and how often do you eat healthy foods?

_____

_____

_____

_____

_____

_____

5.	How much exercise does your body need, what types are best for your body, and how often do you exercise?

_____

_____

_____

_____

_____

_____

6.	Which foods, routines, and activities are bad for your body, and how often do you avoid them?

_____

_____

_____

_____

7.   What clothing sizes, styles, and fabrics are best suited for your body shape and size?

_____

_____

_____

_____

_____

_____

8.   How do you ensure that others treat your body respectfully, and how do you protect your body from being abused by others?

_____

_____

_____

_____

_____

_____

What I've Learned About My Body

During my long journey towards trying to accept and love my body, I've learned some important lessons about it, through the many self-empowerment books, articles, and online medical sources (especially the mayoclinic.org and webmd.com) that I've used. Here are some of the lessons that I've learned that may be helpful to you:

Sleep
   1. In order to wake up feeling rested-- instead of sleep deprived-- I need a *minimum* of seven hours of sleep each night.
   2. I sleep best when there is no background noise in the room.

3. Because my eyes are sensitive to light, I sleep best in a very dark room.
4. Food

Researchers have found that many diseases and illnesses-- including some digestive problems-- are caused by inflammation in the body. As a result of my history of having digestive problems:

1. **My body needs a high-fiber diet.** Therefore, I start my day by drinking home-made green smoothies (consisting of raw green leafy vegetables-- such as collard greens, turnip greens, spinach, kale, beet tops, plus avocado, and fruit). I also drink green tea, and include anti-inflammatory foods, such as parsley and cilantro in my smoothies, and I sprinkle cumin and turmeric in my tea.

2. **My body loves avocado,** so I put it in my smoothies to add healthy fat and protein that will allow the smoothies to keep me satisfied for several hours. Avocado also helps alleviate the symptoms of arthritis, so when I'm feeling achy, I eat extra avocado: usually in the form of home-made guacamole.

3. **Because I'm a vegetarian, my body needs Vitamin B-12 and iron,** so I take a daily multivitamin that contains a good amount of B-12 and iron. A B-12 deficiency can even cause depression, according to Dr. Kelly Brogan, author of *A Mind of Your Own: The Truth About Depression and How Women Can Heal Their Bodies to Reclaim Their Lives*.

4. **In order to minimize the pain that is caused by arthritis, my body needs daily stretching**. Before I get out of bed most mornings, I stretch my back, by slowly sitting up, and touching and holding my toes with both hands for a few minutes.

5. As I already stated, **my body needs lots of anti-inflammatory foods,** so in addition to sprinkling cumin and turmeric in my tea,

and adding cilantro, avocado, and parsley to my smoothies, I sprinkle cumin, turmeric, and onion powder on my food. The Arthritis Foundation's website (http://www.arthritis.org) contains a list of research-proven anti-inflammatory foods and recipes.

6. **My body needs at least seven glasses of water each day** to minimize bloating caused by the high-fiber foods that I eat.

7. **My body has changed over time**. For example, I used to love Peanut Butter-and-Jelly sandwiches, but now I'm allergic to peanuts.

8. Because of my history of having "acid reflux," **I must limit my intake of acidic foods**, including those that I love, such as lemons, oranges, watermelon, cantaloupe, honeydew melon, and tomatoes. Giving up the melons was hard, but I needed to do it.

9. **Refined sugar is my biggest food enemy**. It has been linked to many health problems, including cancer, body-wide inflammation, and negative changes in the brain. Because I wasn't able to eat sugar in moderation, but craved it even more after eating it, through prayer and hard work, I no longer eat any food that contains more than four grams of sugar per serving. However, I'm still working on reducing the amount of salt that I eat each day. My plan is to gradually start eating popcorn that contains less salt, and go back to eating raw and unsalted nuts, because these are the two foods that I eat daily that contain the most salt.

10. The work of **JJ Smith** (a nutritionist and bestselling author of the *10-Day Green Smoothie Cleanse*, and *Green Smoothies for Life*), and **Dr. Joel Fuhrman** (author of *Eat to Live: The Amazing Nutrient-Rich*

Program for Fast and Sustained Weight Loss), has been very helpful to me.

Before I discuss "Exercise," let's continue on this journey to loving and accepting your God-given body with another Personal Growth Exercise.

Personal Growth Exercise: Your Body (Part 5)

1. What are some similarities between your body's needs and mine?

_____

_____

_____

_____

_____

_____

2. What are some differences between what your body needs and what my body needs?

_____

_____

_____

_____

_____

_____

3. What did you learn from the previous section that can move you closer to the goal of learning to love, respect, and accept your God-given body?

_____

_____

_____

_____

Exercise

When we were children, many of us ran, skipped, jumped rope, hula hooped, played Hopscotch, baseball, softball, tether ball, soccer, kick ball, and danced. In other words, we were constantly moving, and had fun while we were moving. Even though we didn't know we were "exercising," this endless chain of activity kept us in shape, and kept our metabolism working properly. Today, many children spend hours sitting in front of the television or playing video games. This, plus the fact that in some schools, children may not have recess or recreational time, has caused childhood obesity rates to increase. Childhood obesity has been linked to many health problems during childhood *and* adulthood. According to the Centers for Disease Control and Prevention (CDC), "Children and adolescents should do 60 minutes (1 hour) or more of physical activity each day."[6]

Just as children may not get enough exercise, the same is true of adults. However, no matter how old we are, our bodies need exercise. I recently met a 91-year-old woman who was power walking at the beach. Adults with health problems can also do chair exercises. If you're wondering how much exercise you need, the following information from the Department of Health and Human Services may be helpful:

- **"Aerobic activity.** Get at least 150 minutes of moderate aerobic activity or 75 minutes of vigorous aerobic activity a week, or a combination of moderate and vigorous activity."
- **"Strength training.** Do strength training exercises for all major muscle groups at least two times a week. Aim to do a single set of each exercise, using a weight or resistance level heavy enough to tire your muscles after about 12 to 15 repetitions."
- **"Moderate aerobic exercise** includes activities such as brisk walking, swimming and mowing the lawn. Vigorous aerobic exercise includes

activities such as running and aerobic dancing. Strength training can include use of weight machines, your own body weight, resistance tubing, resistance paddles in the water, or activities such as rock climbing."

- **"As a general goal**, aim for at least 30 minutes of physical activity every day. If you want to lose weight or meet specific fitness goals, you may need to exercise more. Want to aim even higher? You can achieve more health benefits, including increased weight loss, if you ramp up your exercise to 300 minutes a week."

- **"Reducing sitting time is important**, too. The more hours you sit each day, the higher your risk of metabolic problems, even if you achieve the recommended amount of daily physical activity."

- **"Short or long chunks of time**? Even brief bouts of activity offer benefits. For instance, if you can't fit in one 30-minute walk, try three 10-minute walks instead. What's most important is making regular physical activity part of your lifestyle."[7]

Now that I'm older, and have arthritis, I often have to motivate myself to exercise. Sometimes, my knees, right shoulder, and lower-back are so achy when I wake up, that I really want to skip exercising that day. However, I always find that I feel better and have less pain after I exercise. Each day, I try to walk 8,000 to 10,000 steps, simply by walking in place, around my house, or at the beach. In order to track my steps, I wear a pedometer.

On mornings when I have to get up super early (at three, four, or four-thirty a.m.), I march in place while making my tea, and walk around my kitchen, living room, family room, (or hotel room when travelling) while drinking my smoothies. I also try to walk for 20 minutes at my place of employment. When my shoulders allow it, I also do light weight lifting using five-pound weights, twice a week, as I walk around my house. When my back allows it, I also add about five minutes of hula hooping to my exercise routine. Sometimes, to add variety, I use exercise videos on YouTube. Listening to upbeat gospel music is one of the best ways that I motivate myself to exercise. Before you read and color the Daily Affirmations and drawings for this chapter, please complete a final Personal Growth Exercise.

Personal Growth Exercise: Your Body (Part 6)

1.   How do you feel about exercising, and why do you feel this way?

_____

_____

_____

_____

_____

_____

2.   What are your least favorite types of exercise, and why?

_____

_____

_____

_____

_____

_____

3.   What foods, habits, etc. are you willing to give up in order to treat your body with more respect, and why?

_____

_____

_____

_____

_____

_____

4.   What new practices and routines are you willing to adopt in order to show love and appreciation for your body, and why?

_____

_____

_____

_____

_____

_____

5.   What strategies will you use to help you accept your body type, shape, and size?

_____

_____

_____

_____

_____

_____

6.   Like the man in the story at the beginning of this chapter, at this point can you honestly say "I'm good looking," and mean it? If so, write it and say it out loud five times. If not, explain why you can't.

_____

_____

_____

_____

_____

_____

I AM BEAUTIFUL BECAUSE GOD CREATED ME IN HIS IMAGE. I'M UNIQUE, SPECIAL, AND I'M FINE, JUST AS I AM, AT THIS MOMENT AND STAGE OF MY LIFE.

Art Therapy

Color the following drawings, and as you color them, repeat at least three positive statements about your own body.

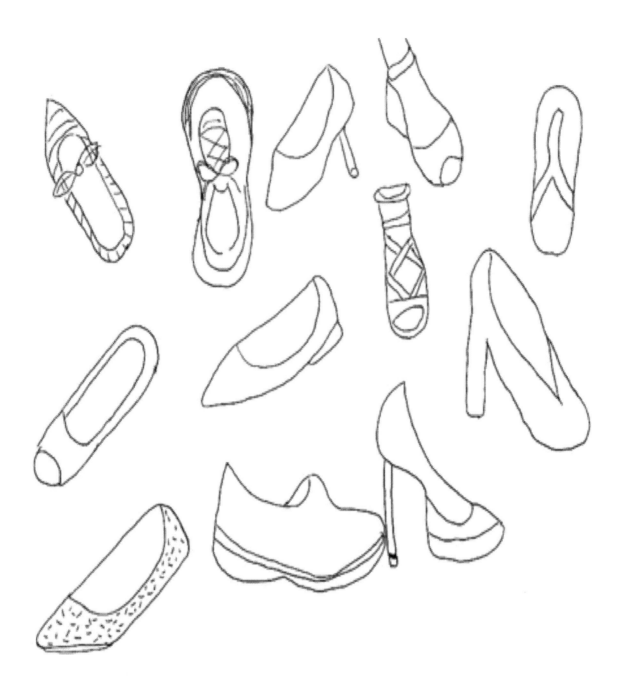

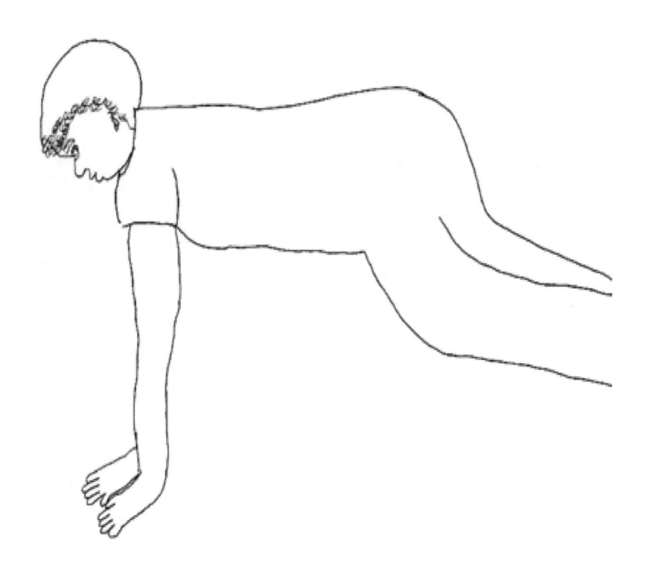

Part Two

The Inside: True Beauty

Chapter Six
Inner Beauty and Why It's More Important

Dear Beautiful!

In Part One, we spent a lot of time, examining *outer beauty* and the messages that we've internalized about our ancestry, physical appearance: skin tone, hair textures, features, body sizes, and body shapes. But in Part Two, the main message that I want to share with you is ***Inner beauty is more important than outer beauty***. Before, I explain my definition of *inner beauty*, I'd like for you to complete another Personal Growth Exercise.

Personal Growth Exercise: Inner Beauty (Part 1)

---

1. Explain why you agree or disagree with the statement "Inner beauty is more important than outer beauty."

_____

_____

_____

_____

_____

_____

2. What is your definition of "inner beauty?"

_____

_____

_____

_____

_____

_____

3. Based on your own definition of "inner beauty," explain whether or not you believe that you are beautiful inside, and the reasons why.

My Definition of Inner Beauty

Have you ever met an attractive woman or handsome man who appeared to be "beautiful" on the outside, but when you got to know this person better, you realized that he or she had an ugly attitude and negative personality? In fact, after being in this person's presence, you felt awful, and when you took a second glance, he or she didn't look so great after all. This person's behavior may have even made you lose all of your previous admiration for him or her. I've met my share of such individuals, and will describe a few of them later. However, here's a related message that I want to emphasize in this chapter:

You can spend a lot of time and money making sure that you look fabulous on the outside. But if you're rotten inside, the stench will leave a stronger impression than your hairstyle, outfit, makeup, nails, or physical beauty etc.

Therefore, my definition of *inner beauty* is:

Inner beauty consists of having Core Beliefs and values that are based on integrity. These Core Beliefs will determine how you behave publicly and privately most of the time.

The Merriam Webster online dictionary (merriam-webster.com) defines "integrity" as "character, decency, morality, goodness, honesty" and "conduct that conforms to an accepted standard of right or wrong." This dictionary also includes a long list of words that are the opposite of "integrity," such as "meanness, crookedness, dishonesty, underhandedness, viciousness, and pervertedness." Now, I'd like for you to complete the next Personal Growth Exercise.

Personal Growth Exercise: Inner Beauty (Part 2)

---

1.   When you think of women who spend a lot of time ensuring that they look great on the outside, but have bad attitudes *most of the time,* which individuals come to mind?

_____

_____

_____

_____

_____

_____

2.   What are some similarities between your definition of "inner beauty" and mine?

_____

_____

_____

_____

_____

_____

3.   How does your definition of "inner beauty" differ from mine?

_____

_____

_____

_____

_____

_____

4.   Write the names of women who meet your definition of "inner beauty."

_____

_____

_____

_____

_____

_____

My Core Beliefs

Like every other individual on this earth, I'm *far* from perfect. Each day, I make mistakes, think mean thoughts, make assumptions about people without getting all of the facts, and sometimes, my attitude and behavior stink. After all, I'm human; I'm not God! In spite of this, each day, I pray for wisdom, strength, guidance, protection, and forgiveness; I also try to learn from my mistakes, and I keep working on empowering and improving myself, in order to become a better person. It's taken me a long time to become the person who I am today. This continuing journey towards self-acceptance and self-love has helped me identify the following main Core Beliefs and values that I want to live by:

1. **God created me in His image,** so I am not a mistake.
2. **God created me for a reason**, which is to use my gifts and talents, especially my writing, drawing, and speaking abilities, to empower others.
3. **I am God's child.**
4. **I should try to treat others with the dignity and respect with which I want to be treated.**
5. **I am not superior or inferior to any individual on this earth,** regardless of the amount of money or education people have, how they look on the outside, or the type of position or job they have.

In the next Personal Growth Exercise, please explain your Core Beliefs.

Personal Growth Exercise: Inner Beauty (Part 3)

1.   What are your main "Core Beliefs?"

_____

_____

_____

_____

_____

_____

2.   What are some similarities between your "Core Beliefs" and mine?

_____

_____

_____

_____

_____

_____

3.   How do your "Core Beliefs" differ from mine?

_____

_____

_____

_____

_____

4.   How do you ensure that your behavior is consistent with your "Core Beliefs" most of the time?

_____

_____

_____

Why Inner Beauty is More Important Than Outer Beauty

Although I know for certain that *inner beauty* is more important than *outer beauty*, I'd be lying if I said that "looks don't matter," because they do, especially for Black women. Just as we often judge others based on how they look, lots of people judge us based on our outer appearance. This is one reason why so many of us grew up believing that we had to be "well dressed" whenever we left home. In spite of this, there are several reasons why *inner beauty* is more important than *outer beauty*. Here are two of them:

1. An accident or tragedy can destroy or alter one's physical appearance in a split second.
2. No matter how much plastic/cosmetic surgery a person may buy, every individual is growing older each day. No amount of surgery can make an 80-year-old woman look like she did when she was 20 years old.

In other words, "None of us can stop the aging process from altering our facial features, skin, and body." However, even though we can't stop ourselves from growing and looking older, we can become more inwardly beautiful as we age, by doing the following:

1. *choosing* to become "works in progress": individuals who adopt Core Beliefs that are based on integrity,

2. making sure that our behavior is consistent with those beliefs, and

3. making a commitment to continue to work on improving our beliefs, personalities, and behavior on an ongoing basis

On the other hand, individuals who devote the majority of their time and attention to only trying to look good on the outside, while failing to cultivate *inner beauty*, won't become more beautiful as they age. They may look decent on the outside for a while, but will continue to have a negative effect on others, as a result of not dealing with their personal issues. These personal issues that produce *inner ugliness*, may consist of (1) a failure to truly know and understand who they really are and who they were created to be; (2) insecurity; (3) jealousy; (4) self-hatred; (5) hatred of others; and (6) low self-esteem. The next section illustrates these points.

Are Haters Always Gon' Hate?

Several years ago, I told my husband, son, sister, mother, and daughters-- Nafissa and NaChe'-- about a huge lie that one or two of my extended family members (two women whom I had previously trusted and respected) had made up, and spread about my husband and me. When I mentioned the lie to one of the two women whom I suspected of spreading it, she laughed and turned it into a joke.

This lie hurt me so much that to this very day, I keep my distance from these women-- who have never apologized-- yet continue to act innocent when they speak to me. When NaChe' heard about the lie, she became very upset. Knowing that several relatives would see the post, she wrote on Facebook, "Haters Gon' Hate!" Since then, I've often thought about her statement "Haters Gon' Hate," because it's related to Core Beliefs and *inner beauty*. Some of the worse stories that I know, pertain to people who fail to do the *inner growth* work that results in behaving with integrity.

Sadly, in various churches that I've attended and even joined, I've met women who "dressed like a million bucks," meaning they looked gorgeous on the outside. However, some of these women were too arrogant to speak, smile, or even nod at me and other women whom they considered to be inferior to them, or whom they viewed as a threat to their fragile self-esteem.

For example, several years ago, I visited a small church in southern California for the first time. Before entering the sanctuary, I went into the restroom. A heavy-set Black woman, who appeared to be in her late 20's or early 30's, was the only other person in the restroom. When I said "hello" to her, if "looks could kill," I'd be dead!

That should've been a warning to me, but it took me five months of attending this church, and having several painful experiences, to realize that the church was run by a clique of "Mean Ole Girl's." Like the woman in the restroom, these women felt threatened by newcomers and outsiders-- especially highly-educated ones-- and they only wanted women whom they could control to attend their church. After experiencing a very public and blatant example of meanness that was fueled by their need to make me "bow down" to them, I eventually came to my senses, and stopped attending that particular church.

One of the worse cases that I've experienced pertaining to a woman who hadn't done her *inner growth* work, involved a former coworker of mine. When I first started working at this particular southeastern university, a 70-ish-year-old Black woman was one of the first individuals to welcome me. After that, she often stopped by my office to see how I was doing. As a newcomer to that university and region, I was so grateful for her friendliness and advice, that I quickly began to view her as a mentor, and someone whom I could trust. Three years later, the truth came out: as it always does, no matter how long it takes.

One day, I received an email from a powerful man at that university. The email was so negative and demeaning that it left me in tears. When I confided in the woman whom I viewed as a mentor, a strange look developed in her eyes. Then, she smiled and said calmly:

I'm going to tell you why *everyone* hates you! Southerners hate Californians. When I use to live in Texas, we would *never* hire a Californian at my old job. If we found out that someone from California was applying for a teaching job, we'd say "Get to the end of the line, with your scraggly hair!" We hated Californians so much that we were actually hoping that an earthquake would knock California into the ocean!

Her words shocked me and hurt my feelings. But after I stopped crying, my eyes "were opened." For the first time, I saw this woman as she really was. Instead of just being a "Mean Ole Girl," she was actually a "Snake-on-Two-Legs." "Mean Ole Girls" have bad attitudes and are unfriendly. "Snakes-on-Two-Legs" smile and pretend to like you, while hiding their true feelings about you.

This old woman looked harmless and innocent on the outside, but inside, she was an evil, poisonous viper who had been smiling in my face while *hating* me all along. I also realized that when I was hired at that university, because of my need to be accepted by my colleagues, I had overlooked some important warning signs. First, I had ignored the uneasiness (gut feeling) that I usually felt in this woman's presence. In hindsight, that feeling was my intuition, warning me about her. Second, my husband had told me that there was something about her that he disliked. Third, this woman usually had something negative to say about other women at the university. On the day when she finally revealed her true colors to me, instead of admitting that *she* hated Californians like me, she placed the blame on *all* Southerners.

Now, whenever, I have a similar experience, I think of a plant that I often saw growing in several southeastern states. The plant consists of a vine that grows in the wild during spring and summer. It produces beautiful lavender-colored flowers in clusters that droop, and remind me of a Weeping Willow Tree.

During my first year living in the southeast, I decided that this lovely-looking plant would be great for our (my husband and my) backyard. However, when I went to a local nursery and described it to a salesman, he said "That plant is a predator! It'll destroy every other plant in your yard, so we don't sell it."

Of course, I was surprised to hear this. How could something so beautiful be so deadly? I was also disappointed that I couldn't have this plant. However, afterwards, each time that I saw that plant growing in wooded areas in southeastern states, I was reminded of the famous quote "Looks can be deceiving." So, the answer to the question "Are haters always gon' hate?" is "YES, if they aren't willing to do the *inner growth* work that we all must do on an ongoing basis. The next Personal Growth Exercise is related to the previous stories.

Personal Growth Exercise: Inner Beauty (Part 4)

1.   What do you think about the stories of the beautiful plant, the "Mean Ole Girls," and the "Snake-on-Two-Legs"?

_____

_____

_____

_____

_____

_____

2.   What similar experiences have you had?

_____

_____

_____

_____

_____

_____

3.   How do you protect yourself from "Mean Ole Girls" and "Snakes-on-Two-Legs"?

_____

_____

_____

_____

_____

_____

4.   Have you ever acted like a "Mean Ole Girl" or a "Snake-on-Two-Legs" out of jealousy, insecurity, and/or low self-esteem? If so, what behaviors did you engage in, who were the victims, and how did the situation(s) end?

_____

_____

_____

_____

_____

5.   What specific things do you do on a regular basis to decrease the chances that you will behave like a "Mean Ole Girl" and "Snake-on-Two-Legs?"

_____

_____

_____

_____

_____

_____

Moving Forward

Because we aren't perfect, at various times from childhood through adulthood, each of us has engaged in behaviors of which we are ashamed. In order to keep these negative behaviors from becoming common practices that will drive others away from us, we must continuously strive to become *inwardly beautiful*. As I previously stated, we can become more *inwardly beautiful* as we age by:

   1. *choosing* to be "works in progress": individuals who adopt Core Beliefs that are based on integrity,

2. making sure that our behavior is consistent with these beliefs, and

3. making a commitment to continue to work on improving our beliefs, personalities, and behavior on an ongoing basis.

The rest of this book is designed to help you continue on this journey, starting with the following Daily Affirmations and Art Therapy.

I AM BEAUTIFUL, BECAUSE GOD CREATED ME IN HIS IMAGE.

I AM WORKING ON BECOMING MORE INWARDLY BEAUTIFUL EACH DAY.

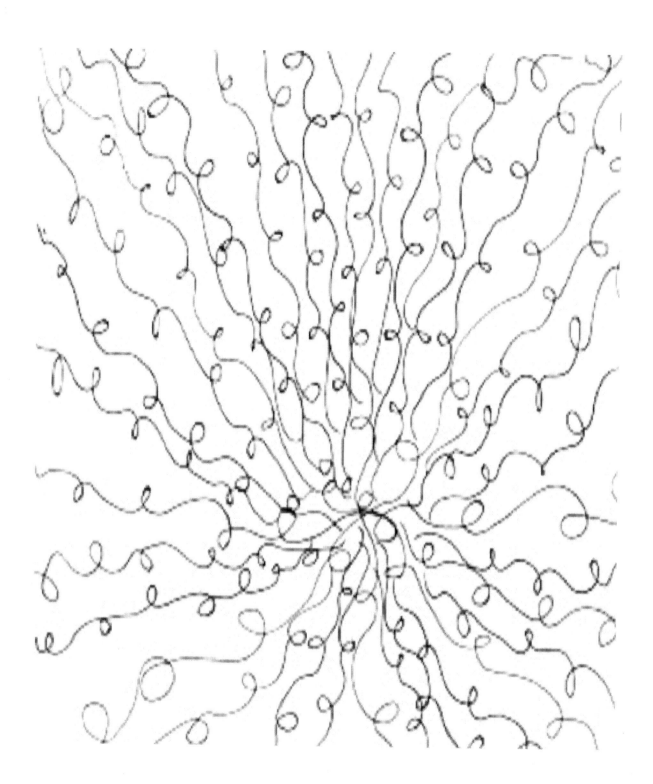

Chapter Seven
Learning to Love and Accept Your Personality

Dear Beautiful!

On October 25, 2017, I started the day with my daily "Prayer-Bible-Study-and Self-Empowerment-Reading-Routine." However, within two hours of reaching my job site, I was disappointed with myself. It all started when I attended a meeting, at which I was required to give a short presentation about my Equity work. As usual, long before the day of the meeting arrived, I prepared an outline of key points to cover, and reviewed the outline several times. I also used my ongoing self-confidence booster: prayer, which is my go-to-strategy for *every* situation that is too big for me to handle alone.

Although I receive many speaking requests, public speaking is never easy for me. The reason is that when I was in seventh grade, a teacher and School Speech Therapist told me that I had a *speech impediment*. Afterwards, the therapist would call me out of my English class twice each week, to work with me on my lisp. He claimed that I had a problem pronouncing words that ended in the letter "s" and that began with "th" properly. Even though I never believed that I had a speech impediment, this diagnosis had a negative effect on my self-esteem.

Since then, I've always been self-conscious about my speaking abilities. Therefore, no matter how large or small the audience that I'm invited to speak to will be, before the day of the engagement arrives, I spend lots of time practicing my speech and praying for clarity of thought, clarity of speech, wisdom, and courage. Prayer, and especially *answered prayer*, gives me the courage to speak clearly, boldly, and confidently in every situation. So, if I prayed and prepared for that meeting in October ahead of time, why did I feel so disappointed afterwards? Before I share the rest of the story, I'd like for you to complete the following Personal Growth Exercise.

Personal Growth Exercise: Your Personality (Part 1)

1. In your opinion, why did I feel so disappointed with myself after that meeting?

_____

_____

_____

_____

_____

2. Describe a time when you were disappointed with yourself and the reasons why.

_____

_____

_____

_____

_____

_____

3. When you feel disappointed with yourself, what strategies do you use in order to "keep it moving," instead of wallowing in misery?

_____

_____

_____

_____

_____

_____

Two Crucial Questions

After spending most of the day feeling disappointed with myself, I had to do two things: First, I had to decide "Am I going to continue to feel like a failure, or am I going to let go of the negative thoughts that caused me to feel bad?" Second, I had to figure out *why* I was so upset with myself, because I couldn't really get over the disappointment until I did this. As I started examining what actually happened during the meeting and why I felt so disappointed, the answers soon became clear to me.

What Happened During the Meeting?

During the meeting, as I began to describe one of my key points-- a work-related issue that had frustrated me and made my Equity work more difficult than necessary for nearly a year-- I became emotional. Pain that I'd been suppressing, slowly grew inside of me and reached my vocal chords. As I spoke to the group, in spite of my efforts to hold back tears, my coworkers could tell that I was upset. After the meeting, the other two women who had been present said that as I was speaking, they had wanted to give me a hug. I appreciated their encouragement, but still felt bad for the rest of the day.

The Real Causes

Later, when I tried to figure out why I felt so awful about becoming emotional during the meeting, I realized the following:

1. Although everyone has emotions, and God gave us emotions for a reason, I was "beating myself up" for being human.

2. As only one of two Black women in the entire company, I was also worried about being labelled as "weak," because I'm very familiar with the research that says that women who cry in the workplace are often viewed this way.

3. My life-long struggle to accept my God-given personality was really the main cause of my disappointment.

In this chapter, you'll learn more about this struggle, and lessons that I've learned. You'll also have opportunities to examine your beliefs about "'personality," especially your own. This is important, because as Black women, just as we've been bombarded with negative messages about our *outer beauty*, the same is true of our personalities. So, by the time that you reach the end of this chapter, I hope that you'll be further along the path of accepting and loving your God-given personality. This is needed in order to develop *inner beauty*. Now, let's continue with another Personal Growth Exercise.

Personal Growth Exercise: Your Personality (Part 2)

1.   Describe your personality.

_____

_____

_____

_____

_____

_____

2.   What messages have you heard about your personality, from whom have you heard them, and how have the messages affected you?

_____

_____

_____

_____

_____

_____

3.   How do you feel about your personality, and why do you feel this way?

_____

_____

_____

_____

_____

_____

4.   If you could change one thing about your personality, what would it be, and why would you change it?

_____

_____

_____

_____

_____

_____

5.   Which of the following words describe your personality most of the time? Which would you like to add to your personality, and which would you like to get rid of?

feisty	quiet	talkative	thoughtful	sensitive
outgoing	suspicious	outspoken	assertive	meticulous
strong	undermining	private	moody	generous
curious	shy	aggressive	passive	negative
serious	loner	friendly	bold	timid
jealous	backstabber	supportive	loyal	honest
polite	sincere	humorous	uplifting	cheerful
fun-loving				

_____

_____

_____

_____

_____

_____

My Ongoing Struggle to Accept and Love My Personality

For most of my life, I wanted to have the personality of my

younger sister Tammie, who died in 1995. From the time that she was in elementary school, Tammie's brilliance impressed teachers and most adults. During childhood, some of the kids in our neighborhood nicknamed her "Scholar." She was a straight "A" student, well behaved, and eventually graduated from law school. In fact, shortly before she died, Tammie was studying for the California Bar Exam. She made such a great impression on her law professors, that they named a scholarship after her. Although Tammie's intelligence impressed people, her personality was the main thing that I admired about her. Tammie was a loner and a very quiet person. She minded her own business, and kept her emotions under control most of the time. Whenever someone tried to "get under her skin," Tammie would usually laugh and act like she wasn't bothered.

Unlike Tammie, I've always had trouble hiding my emotions. In kindergarten, I cried so much that the teacher often made me sit in the restroom that was connected to the classroom. In first grade, I cried so often, that at the end of the school year, the teacher told my mother, "Gail is too emotionally immature for second grade." Flunking first grade was one of the greatest blows to my self-esteem.

At the same time that I was struggling at school, Tammie was thriving. She was so advanced academically that her third-grade teacher viewed her as a genius, and wanted her to skip a grade. After flunking first grade, I realized that if I didn't stop crying at school, I would never make it to second grade. The problem was that I still had a lot of painful emotions bottled up inside that needed an outlet. So, I became an "excessive talker," whom teachers soon viewed as a "behavior problem."

From childhood onward, negative labels followed me: "dummy," "Miss Motless," the "N Word," "speech impaired," "blackie," "man voice," "ugly," "poor," "too sensitive," "big nose," "long head," and the list goes on. Today, as a result of my Equity work, a more recent label that has been applied to me is "Angry Black Woman," from haters, racists, and underminers who mistake my passion for anger. With all of the negative labels that I've heard about myself, it's no wonder that I've struggled with low self-esteem and had difficulty accepting my God-given personality: Words and labels do hurt and affect how we view ourselves.

Defining My Personality

Because of the negative labels that have been placed on me, it's taken me a long time to truly understand what *is* and *isn't* true about my personality. For example, at my current job, I recently took a company-required personality test, which stated:

> Gail is a confident, independent self-starter with competitive drive, initiative, a sense of urgency, and the ability to make decisions and take responsibility for them. She can react and adjust quickly to changing conditions, and come up with ideas for dealing with them. Her drive is purposeful, directed at getting things done quickly. She responds positively and actively to challenge and pressure, and she has confidence in her ability to handle novel problems and people. She is an outgoing, poised person, a lively and enthusiastic communicator, tending to be a little more authoritative than persuasive in her style. Gail talks briskly, with assurance and conviction and is a stimulating influence on others, while being firm, direct, and self-assured in dealing with them.
>
> Her work pace is distinctly faster-than-average. She learns and takes action quickly. On the other hand, she will become impatient and restless working repetitively with routine details or structured work, will delegate such work if her position permits, and will follow up, focusing on completion and accomplishment, rather than how things were done. With an interest in other people and their development, Gail will delegate authority, limiting such delegation to people in whom she has high levels of confidence, and following up with pressure for timely results. She makes decisions about people and situations quickly. She assesses what's generally going on, and rather than exhaustive research, pulls together the information she has and takes action forcefully. She's confident in her assumptions about any missing information, and

is comfortable acting even in the absence of complete information. For Gail, continual progress towards the general goal is more important than always being exactly on track; she's flexible and will make course corrections as necessary, when the time arises. Sure of herself, Gail sets high standards of achievement for herself and others and looks for opportunities to compete and to win. Venturesome, she is stimulated by new challenges and situations, and is generally driving herself and others to new horizons. She is ambitious both for herself and for the business which employs her.

When I read this summary of my test results, I was pleasantly surprised. Not only did I agree with almost all of the results, but I was actually pleased at the way in which I was described. Accepting, agreeing with, and being pleased with this description was truly a sign that I've made progress towards understanding and accepting my God-given personality. The next Personal Growth Exercise allows you to share your opinions about the previous section.

| Personal Growth Exercise: Your Personality (Part 3) |

1.   Based on the above description, what are some similarities between your personality and mine?

_____

_____

_____

_____

_____

_____

2.   What are some differences between your personality and mine?

_____

_____

_____

_____

Owning, Accepting, and Loving My Personality

As I explained previously, I use to reject my personality, because I believed that my sister Tammie's personality was much better than mine. In addition to that, my grandmother use to say, "Now, be sweet," and I always felt that *being sweet* was the same as being quiet, and not standing up to people when necessary. I really wish that I had taken the time to ask my grandmother what her definition of "sweet" was when she was alive, because I always felt that I didn't fit it. Over time, however, through my own self-empowerment work, I've learned the following facts that have really helped me learn to own, accept, and begin to love my personality:

1. **God likes color, diversity, and uniqueness.** If He had wanted us all to have the same hair texture, features, body sizes, shapes, skin tone, *and personalities*, He would've created us to look and act in identical ways.

2. **My personality is no better or worse than any other God-given personality**.

3. **Because no one is perfect, like all personalities, my personality has strengths and areas that need improvement.**

4. **Many of the women "trailblazers" whom I most admire, such as Sojourner Truth, Harriet Tubman, Ida B. Wells, Maya Angelou, and Maxine Waters, had/have some of the same personality traits that I have.**

5. **In order to do the Equity and Empowerment work that I've been created to do, I need to be feisty, courageous, and outspoken.**

For the next Personal Growth Exercise, I'd like for you to read several scenarios, and explain how you would handle each one.

> **Personal Growth Exercise: Your Personality (Part 4)**

1.   What would you do if you were walking down a street, and a teenager whom you didn't know, asked you for money?

_____

_____

_____

_____

_____

2.   What would you do if the grocery store cashier who was ringing up your items, told you that he was recovering from the flu, yet kept coughing while touching the fresh fruit that you were trying to buy?

_____

_____

_____

_____

_____

3.   What would you do if you saw an adult man pressuring two teenagers to give him their cellphone numbers?

_____

_____

_____

_____

_____

4.   What would you do, if you were sitting on an airplane, and the stranger sitting next to you, kept coughing in your direction without covering his mouth?

_____

_____

_____

_____

_____

_____

5.   What would you do if one of your coworkers telephoned you three times and used passive-aggressive tactics to insult you, yet each time you saw him at work, he smiled and acted pleasant?

_____

_____

_____

_____

_____

_____

6.   What would you do if you were trying to take a nap on an airplane, but couldn't sleep, because the two strangers who were sitting next to you-- a Black man and a Latino teenager-- were bragging about selling illegal drugs? Furthermore, the adult was even giving the teen tips on how to earn more money while selling drugs at his high school.

_____

_____

_____

_____

_____

_____

**How I Handled Each Situation,
and the Related Life Lessons That I Learned**

The questions that I asked you to respond to in the previous section, were actual situations that I've experienced. Below, I describe how I handled each situation and explain the lessons that I learned.

The Boy With the "Pointed Head"

Long ago, when I was a struggling college undergraduate who could barely make ends meet each month, I was walking to a bus stop in downtown Los Angeles when a boy, who appeared to be 13 or 14 years old, approached me. He said, "Ma'am, can you give me a dollar?" I replied, "Little boy, I don't have a dollar to give you." Then he asked, "What would you do if I snatched your purse?"

I was so upset that he had the nerve to imply that he'd take the little money that I had, that without thinking of the consequences, I said, "Boy, if you snatch my purse, I'll knock that point off of your head!" (I was referring to the odd shape of his head.) In a split second, the teen pulled a knife out of his pocket, and calmly asked, "What did you say?" I started running as fast as I could. When I got far enough away from him, and looked back, I saw that he was laughing so hard that he hadn't bothered to chase me. **The lesson that I learned and am still trying to learn is that** *it pays to think before I speak*.

The Coughing Cashier

In the situation involving the grocery-store cashier who told me that he was recovering from the flu, yet kept coughing and touching the fruit that I was trying to buy, I simply said, "I've changed my mind. I don't want to buy that fruit." Although he looked confused, I spoke up because my health was more important to me than what he thought about me. **The related lesson is that** *it's better to speak up than to end up getting sick, as a result of someone else's inconsiderate behavior.*

The Adult "Predator"

The situation regarding the adult who was pressuring the two teen girls to give him their cellphone numbers occurred in 2017, when my husband and I were at the beach one day. As we were watching the sunset, we couldn't help but see and hear the man repeatedly asking the girls for their phone numbers. When one of them finally gave in, he dialed the number on his cellphone. When the call didn't go through, the man made it clear that he knew she had given him the wrong number. After pressuring her to give him the correct one, the girl gave in.

When the man left, I warned the girls to be careful, because I suspected that he was dangerous. They told me that they thought he was "scary" and "creepy," but "just wanted to be nice." I said that being "nice" could result in them being raped, "sex-trafficked," and murdered. I also warned them to be very careful as they were leaving the beach, because the man might follow them home. They were very grateful that I shared my concerns with them. **The related lesson is that** *being safe and self-protective are more important than trying to be "nice."*

The Rude Airplane Seatmate

In the case of the man on the airplane, who kept coughing in my direction without covering his mouth, I finally asked him politely, "Sir, would you mind covering your mouth when you cough?" Although he looked surprised, after that, he did try to cover his mouth when he coughed, though he sometimes forgot to do so. **The main lesson is that** *some people need to be taught or reminded to do basic things that others take for granted.*

The Passive-Aggressive-Bullying Coworker

After realizing that talking and trying to reason with him was a total waste of time, I used three strategies to deal with my bullying coworker: I blocked his number so that he could never telephone or text me again; I started avoiding him "like the plague" at work and "feeding him with a long-handled professional spoon." This means that I decided to only interact with him when it was absolutely necessary. I also put him on a very special prayer list that I reserve for my haters. **The main lesson that I learned is that** *what Shakespeare said is still true: "One may smile and smile and still be a villain."*

The Bragging Drug Dealers

The situation involving the adult male and teenage boy who were bragging about selling illegal drugs, occurred when I was on a flight from Houston, Texas to San Diego, California in November 2017. No matter how hard I tried to sleep and mind my own business, I couldn't help but hear their conversation, and what I heard really bothered me.

Finally, I told them about my two brothers who died under tragic circumstances (one died in prison; the other was murdered) after being crack addicts for most of their lives. I also told these strangers that if they didn't change their lives, their stories would also have bad endings. "After all, the jails are full of Black and Latino males, just like you!" I said. They listened politely, and the teen actually thanked me. When the airplane landed, he hugged me three times and said that I was "an angel." I told him that I'd be praying for both of them to change their ways. **The related lesson is that** *when moral indignation rises up inside of me, my personality won't allow me to remain silent.*

The next Personal Growth Exercise will allow you to share your thoughts about the previous section.

Personal Growth Exercise: Your Personality (Part 5)

---

1.   What do you think about how I handled each situation, and the related lessons that I shared?

_____

_____

_____

_____

_____

_____

2.   Describe a time when you were fearful about speaking up, the reasons for your fearfulness, and explain how you handled the situation.

_____

_____

_____

_____

_____

_____

Continuing On Your Journey to Inner Beauty

Learning to accept, love, and appreciate your God-given personality is an important part of the *inner beauty* work that we all must do. It requires ongoing work. Before you complete the last Personal Growth Exercise in this chapter, read the Daily Affirmations, and complete the Art Therapy, I'm sharing some personality-related strategies that I hope will be helpful.

Seven Personality-Acceptance Strategies

1. Regardless of your personality type, **strive to behave with integrity** and in ways that will cause you to like and respect the person whom you see in the mirror each day.

2. **Be authentic**, and not phony or a follower.

3. **Give yourself permission to be human,** which includes understanding that you'll never be perfect.

4. **Forgive yourself** at the end of each day.

5. **Continue to work on areas of your personality** that need improvement.

6. **Don't let haters, "Mean Ole Girls," and "Snakes-on-Two-Legs" push your buttons.** In other words, don't let their attitudes and behaviors compel you to behave in ways that'll make *you* look bad.

7. Regardless of your personality type, whenever possible, **try to be polite, respectful, and treat people as you would like to be treated.**

The next Personal Growth Exercise can help you move forward on your journey *to inner beauty.*

Personal Growth Exercise: Your Personality (Part 6)

1.   What does your personality need in order to be healthy, and why?

_____

_____

_____

_____

_____

_____

2.   What new routines and practices are you willing to adopt in order to protect, love, and appreciate your God-given personality?

_____

_____

_____

_____

_____

_____

3.   When do you plan to begin these new practices, and how will you hold yourself accountable for protecting, loving, and appreciating your God-given personality?

_____

_____

_____

_____

_____

_____

I AM BEAUTIFUL, BECAUSE GOD CREATED ME IN HIS IMAGE. GOD GAVE ME THE PERSONALITY THAT HE WANTED ME TO HAVE. I LOVE MY PERSONALITY.

Chapter Eight
Building Your Self-Esteem and Improving Your Self-Image

Dear Beautiful!

By now, you know about my ongoing struggle to accept my outer appearance and personality. You also know that from childhood onward, I internalized many negative messages about myself. These messages affected how I viewed myself, treated myself, and the value that I placed on myself. In other words, you know that for most of my life, I've had a huge inferiority complex, felt that other people were better than me, and that I've had to fight *low self-esteem*. However, I thank God that I've come a mighty long way from being that college student who believed that I was ugly, and that dark-skinned Black women like me, were cursed. Today, I know that I am blessed and highly-favored: good enough, smart enough, gifted, talented, *inwardly* and *outwardly beautiful*, and I have *high self-esteem* most of the time.

In the previous chapter, we focused on *personality*, which is related to how you behave and handle situations most of the time. In this chapter, we'll focus on *self-esteem*, which is how you view yourself and the value that you place on yourself most of the time. Having *low self-esteem* means that you have a negative opinion of your self-worth and value, and think of yourself in negative ways most of the time. Having *high self-esteem* means that you believe that you are a valuable individual, and you think in positive ways about yourself most of the time.

Like personality acceptance, developing healthy self-esteem is a necessary part of the *inner-growth* process, because if you don't believe that you are valuable, it'll be difficult for you to become *inwardly beautiful*. Remember that *inner beauty* means that most of the time, we behave according to our Core Beliefs. Hopefully, these Core Beliefs are based on integrity (doing the right things privately and in public). This keeps us from acting ugly, hateful, and from becoming "Mean Ole Girls" and "Snakes-on-Two-Legs." Before I continue, I'd like for you to complete another Personal Growth Exercise.

Personal Growth Exercise: Your Self-Esteem (Part 1)

1.   On a scale of 1 to 10, with 1 meaning "not valuable at all," and 10 meaning "extremely valuable," how valuable do you consider yourself to be?

_____

_____

_____

_____

_____

_____

2.   Explain why you gave yourself that rating.

_____

_____

_____

_____

_____

3.   In terms of your "self-esteem" (what you think about yourself most of the time), with 1 meaning "low self-esteem," and 10 meaning "extremely high self-esteem," what rating would you give yourself, and why?

_____

_____

_____

_____

_____

4.   If your closest family members and friends were asked to rate your level of "self-esteem," what rating would most of them give you, and why would they do so?

_____

_____

_____

_____

_____

5.   Now, review all of your answers. Based on what they reveal, explain why you believe that you have "high self-esteem" or "low self-esteem."

_____

_____

_____

_____

_____

_____

Some Causes of Low Self-Esteem for Black Women

In *A Brighter Day: How Parents Can Help African American Youth*, I devoted an entire chapter to the topic of *self-esteem*. That chapter, titled "Nothing from Nothing Leaves Nothing: Why We Need Healthy Self-Esteem and Self-Respect," includes the definitions of self-esteem, causes of low self-esteem for Black folks, several true stories, and self-esteem-building strategies. Some of the causes that I described are:

- ongoing negative messages that we receive from the media and others
- stereotypes
- racism

- shaming
- dysfunctional family practices, and
- negative generational cycles being passed down

Why Having Low Self-Esteem is Dangerous

In *A Brighter Day*, I also stated that having low self-esteem is extremely dangerous. For example, having low self-esteem:

- will determine how you treat yourself
- will determine how you view and treat others
- will determine how others view and treat you
- will increase your chances of being taken advantage of by abusive individuals, including users/opportunists, control freaks, manipulators, predators, sociopaths, and cult leaders.

Examples of Women with Low Self-Esteem and the Consequences

In *A Brighter Day*, I shared several examples of women who had low self-esteem and the related consequences. Now, I'd like to share three new examples. **These stories are disturbing, so feel free to skip them and the next Personal Growth Exercise if you'd prefer.**

The Highly-Successful Woman

In 2017, the U.S. was rocked by numerous scandals involving highly-successful politicians, entertainers, journalists, and other men who were accused of sexual misconduct. Some of the victims were children when the alleged abuse occurred. At the time when they were victimized, others were young women who were trying to get their careers started. My heart went out to every single victim, and each story upset me. However, I was happy that the truth was finally coming out about so many powerful men who had gotten away with sexual misconduct for so long.

Out of all of the stories that I heard, the one that disturbed me the most, involved a highly-successful woman. According to numerous media reports, the alleged victim was a producer at a major television network. One day, the most popular morning news host at the station, summoned her to his office. When she arrived, this married man and father, locked the door and ordered her to unbutton her blouse. Then, the man raped her so violently that she lost consciousness.

Afterwards, the story was covered up by the network. The alleged rapist remained on the air and continued to earn millions of dollars each year. To me, the saddest part of this story is that the woman blamed herself, instead of the sociopathic maniac who attacked her! Today, I still wonder why she placed so little value on her self-worth that she would blame herself for the evil that was done to her.

The next two stories are based on episodes of one of my favorite television shows, "Lauren Lake's Paternity Court." Unlike similar television program hosts, Judge Lake doesn't exploit the individuals who are seeking to prove the paternity of their children. Instead, Judge Lake, who is also an author, uses her television program to help women become stronger, wiser, and better individuals, by encouraging them to work on their self-esteem.

The Teen Mom

A recent episode of "Lauren Lake's Paternity Court" featured a Black teenager who was trying to prove that another teenager had fathered her child. The alleged father said that he didn't believe that he was the child's father, because of the mother's past behavior. It turned out that he and another teen had had a "threesome" with her. In other words, the girl had agreed to have sex with both males at the same time. Later, when the girl announced that she was pregnant, neither male believed that he was the father.

When Judge Lake read the DNA Test Results, it turned out that the girl's threesome partners had been right: Neither was the father. After hearing this, she burst into tears and said, "I'm just a whore who doesn't know who her baby's daddy is." This story reminded me that many teens and women who have low self-esteem, allow themselves to be taken advantage of. The women may be looking for love, but their partners may only be seeking sexual gratification.

The Woman with Seven Children

Another recent episode of "Lauren Lake's Paternity Court," featured a woman who was trying to prove that a certain man was her child's father. Unlike the teenage girl in the previous story, this woman had seven children by three different males. As the story unfolded, it became clear that she had been leaving her children home alone at night, in order to drive long distances to sleep with a man whom she'd met on the Internet.

When the DNA Test Results revealed that her "Long Distance Lover" wasn't her baby's father, all I could think of was the danger that she put her children in, each time that she left them home alone at night. A predator could've entered her home and assaulted those children. The house could've caught on fire, or one of the children could've gotten injured or become seriously ill. In my opinion, this was another example of a woman with low self-esteem who was looking for love from a man who didn't value or respect her, instead of making the wellbeing of her children her top priority.

Personal Growth Exercise: Your Self-Esteem (Part 2)

---

1.   What do you think about the three stories?

_____

_____

_____

_____

_____

_____

2.   Have you ever blamed yourself for something that wasn't your fault? If so, what happened, why did you blame yourself, and who was the person who deserved the blame?

_____

_____

_____

_____

_____

3.   Have you ever allowed yourself to be taken advantage of as a result of "low self-esteem?" If so, what did you learn from this experience that can help you become more self-protective?

_____

_____

_____

_____

_____

_____

How I Improved My Self-Esteem

In *A Brighter Day,* I explained how I improved my self-esteem. Here's a summary of what I said:

Since I have to live with Gail 24 hours a day seven days a week, I might as well learn to love, accept, and nurture the person that I spend more time with than any other person on the face of this earth. The result of this long process has truly helped me to become my own best friend and to realize that I am not the person that so many people tried to convince me that I was.

I am a child of God. I am a good wife. I am a good mother. I am a good great aunt, and was a good foster parent to my great niece who was living with me when I started writing this book. I am a good teacher. I am a good role model. I have a heart that is determined to use the gifts, talents, and opportunities that God has given me to try to make this world a better place. And when life, and toxic and jealous people try to convince me that I am ugly, worthless, too black, too fat or too skinny, not smart enough, not good enough, and inferior, I can counter all of those negative attacks with the truth, and the truth always sets me free![1]

Six Ways That You Can Improve Your Self-Esteem

The following strategies that I've used during my own *inner growth journey*, may be useful to you.

1. Make sure that your Core Beliefs include positive statements about your value and self-worth.

2. Identify your "Real Enemies." For example, I learned that fear, insecurity, and trying to be accepted by the wrong people were problems that contributed to my low self-esteem.

3. Know how to fight your enemies. In terms of fear, insecurity, and trying to be accepted by the wrong people, prayer and consuming "spiritual food" (which I'll say more about in the next chapter), have been the most powerful weapons for me. Reading Bible scriptures that remind me that I am "fearfully and wonderfully made," loved, accepted, and made in God's image always helps me remember who I really am.

4. Accept the fact that some folks, including some of your relatives, aren't meant to be your friends, or in your life for long. Reminding myself of my Core Beliefs, and remembering that when people reject me, it's a warning that they aren't meant to be in my life have been helpful strategies for me. In fact, I often think of what Kerry Shook, a television pastor, once said: "Rejection is God's protection!" This makes it easier for me not to take it personally when people dislike me as a result of their own issues, stemming from a failure to do their own *inner* *growth* work.

5. When people try to convince you that something is wrong with you, always examine the source and the motives, especially when individuals use the words "all" and "everybody." For example, when I was working on my doctorate, another Black woman, whom I considered to be a friend, was a doctoral student at the same university. One day, she told me, "All of the professors hate you!" After I dried my tears and got over my shock, I realized that she was jealous that I was working at a faster pace than she was. Using the same "feeding her with a long-handled-professional-spoon" approach that I use for workplace, church place, and haters in other places, I distanced myself from her. I also continued to work hard, and earned my doctorate years before she earned hers. But the real proof that she was lying all along, was that three years after I earned my doctorate, those very same professors who, according to this woman, hated me, hired me as an Assistant Professor. The best part was that when I became an Assistant Professor at that university, my "frenemy" was still a doctoral student.

6. Accept your God-given personality, and continue to work on the aspects of it that need improvement.

In the next chapter, I share additional inner growth strategies, but now, I'd like for you to complete another Personal Growth Exercise, read the Daily Affirmations, and enjoy the Art Therapy exercises.

Personal Growth Exercise: Your Self-Esteem Part 3

---

1.   In the past, what strategies have helped you improve your "self-esteem?"

_____

_____

_____

_____

_____

_____

2.   Which individuals in your life help you to have "high self-esteem," and how do they help you?

_____

_____

_____

_____

_____

3.   Which individuals in your life are harmful to your "self-esteem," and what tactics do they use in order to make you feel bad about yourself?

_____

_____

_____

_____

_____

4.   What additional strategies do you plan to use in order to continue to improve your "self-esteem?"

_____

_____

_____

_____

_____

5.   Write a "Self-Esteem-Building" song, poem or paragraph that includes all of the things that are wonderful about you. Read it at least once a week, and as you continue on your *inner growth journey,* add new information to it on a regular basis.

_____

_____

_____

_____

_____

I AM BEAUTIFUL, BECAUSE GOD CREATED ME IN HIS IMAGE.

I AM NOT INFERIOR TO ANYONE.

I AM EXTREMELY VALUABLE!

Chapter Nine
The Importance of Self-Care and Self-Protection

Dear Beautiful!

In a previous chapter, I wrote about the importance of making healthy food choices, and getting enough exercise and sleep. In this chapter, I share additional *self-care and self-protection* strategies. Self-care and self-protection are crucial components of the *inner growth journey*, because they are indicators of how you treat yourself, and how others will treat you. They also enable you to protect yourself from "Mean Ole Girls," "Snakes-on-Two-Legs," and stressors that can cause you to behave in ways that conflict with your Core Beliefs. By the end of this chapter, I hope that you'll be much closer to becoming your closest best friend.

Now, let's continue on the *inner growth journey* with a story that I recently read about the late Nina Simone, a famous Black singer. This story emphasizes why it's so vital for us to be self-protective, by engaging in ongoing self-care. **The story is disturbing, so, feel free to skip it and the Personal Growth Exercise that follows.**

Nina Simone

In 2016, I read an interesting biography of Nina Simone, who grew up in North Carolina. As one of the youngest children in a large family, Simone had a good relationship with her father. However, she believed that her mother, a travelling preacher who was often away from home, never really accepted her. For the rest of her life, this belief affected Simone's self-image and self-esteem in negative ways.

Over time, Simone moved to New York, and became a famous singer and pianist. Her popularity eventually grew to the point that she was invited to perform in Africa, Europe, and throughout the U.S. One of her most legendary songs, "To Be Young, Gifted and Black," became a Civil Rights Era classic. However, although she was extremely talented, wealthy, and famous, Simone never overcame the low self-esteem and poor self-image that she developed in childhood. Therefore, for most of her life, she was unhappy, and labelled as a "difficult person." Her failure to be self-protective and to make her own wellbeing top priorities, also caused her to attract and tolerate bad relationships.

Simone's first husband was an opportunist, who took advantage of her financially. Her second husband, a police officer, almost murdered her. To me, the most disturbing fact about her second marriage is that the second husband almost killed her *before* she married him. While they were dating, he beat, tortured, raped, and held her hostage. Although he clearly showed Simone that he was a sadistic "Snake-on-Two-Legs," after he apologized, and begged her forgiveness, Simone not only gave him another chance, but she actually married him, and had a daughter by him.[1]

Like the story that I shared in the previous chapter, about the television producer who blamed herself for being raped by an evil coworker, Simone's story is a reminder that a person can have lots of money, become professionally successful, and even become famous, but if the *inner growth* work hasn't been done, that person can live and die in misery. In the next Personal Growth Exercise, please share your thoughts about Simone's story and a related topic.

Personal Growth Exercise: Self-Care and Self-Protection (Part 1)

1.   What do you think about the Nina Simone story that I shared?

_____

_____

_____

_____

_____

_____

2.   Have you ever given a "Snake-on-Two-Legs" another chance? If so, who was the "snake," why did you do it, what happened, and what did you learn from the experience?

_____

_____

_____

_____

_____

_____

Why Self-Care and Self-Protection Are Top Priorities for Me

In the *personality* chapter, I shared an excerpt from a personality test that I took at work. Some of my personality traits that the test revealed were: "confident, independent, self-starter, competitive, faster-than-average-work-pace, high achiever, ambitious, outgoing, poised, restless, and impatient." However, while it's true that I possess all of these characteristics, the test didn't reveal the two most essential parts of my personality: *empathetic* and *highly sensitive*.

Many years ago, my mother told me that she cried throughout her entire pregnancy with me. So, it's no wonder that I'm a very sensitive person. As I mentioned earlier, when I was in elementary school, I cried so often that I "flunked" first grade. Although I've always been a sensitive person, I never really understood that being *highly sensitive* is one of my most dominant personality traits. I also didn't know that I am an *empath*.

Being a highly sensitive person means that situations, events, and behaviors that may not bother others, may bother me. For example, too much noise, bright lights, crowds, public places, and especially "mess and drama" that others may not even notice, can be overwhelming and stressful for me.

In her bestselling book *The Highly Sensitive Person: How to Thrive When the World Overwhelms You*, Dr. Elaine N. Aron, said that highly sensitive people have a "sensitive nervous system," are "aware of subtleties in [their]surroundings," are "easily overwhelmed when they have been out in a highly stimulating environment for too long," and are "bombarded by sights and sounds. . . ." She also said that this sensitivity is probably inherited. Her book contains many wonderful strategies that highly sensitive individuals can use to protect themselves.[2]

The *Merriam Webster Dictionary* (merriam-webster.com) defines *empathy* as "the action of understanding, being aware of, being sensitive to, and vicariously experiencing the feelings, thoughts, and experiences of another." A person who is *empathetic* is "considerate, tenderhearted, compassionate, sensitive, sympathetic, and understanding" (merriam-webster.com). In *The Empathy Trap: Understanding Antisocial Personalities*, Dr. Jane McGregor and Tim McGregor said, "Empaths are ordinary people who are highly perceptive and insightful, and belong to the 40 percent of human beings who sense when something's not right (those who respond to their 'gut instinct')."[3] Therefore, being an empath means that I am a very empathetic person. When I pay attention to my subconscious, I can detect and pick up subtle clues from people and situations that others may miss.

My failure to realize that being a highly sensitive person and an empath are the strongest parts of my personality has caused a lot of problems for me. Consequently, I've been in far too many places and around too many individuals who created a lot of mess, stress, and drama for me: the very things that I now do my best to avoid. Sadly, because empaths feel sorry for people who appear to be in need, they also tend to attract the worst kinds of "Snakes-on-Two-Legs": sociopaths (people with Antisocial Personality Disorder) and Malignant Narcissists. These two groups appear to be very charming, nice, and decent. However, throughout history, the most destructive political, religious, and workplace leaders, as well as serial killers, and serial rapists have fit into one of these two categories. Sociopaths and Malignant Narcissists tend to:

- take advantage of others
- be verbally, emotionally, and/or physically abusive

- not care about anyone's feelings and needs except for their own
- destroy everyone in their path, and
- "blame the victim" instead of themselves for their evil deeds

They're also unwilling to do the *inner growth* work that we all need to do. For anyone who has ever been targeted by a sociopath or Malignant Narcissist, the McGregors' book, *The Empathy Trap* . . . is a must-read.

The good news is that my failure to understand the pros and cons of being highly sensitive and an empath has taught me some unforgettable life lessons that have made me stronger, wiser, more discerning, and definitely more self-protective. Now, before these "snakes" can slither up to me and "bite me," I can spot sociopaths and Malignant Narcissists more quickly. Before I share those lessons, I'd like for you to complete the next Personal Growth Exercise.

Personal Growth Exercise: Self-Care and Self-Protection (Part 2)

1.   What patterns or themes have you noticed in your life, concerning the types of problems that you tend to have?

_____

_____

_____

_____

_____

_____

2.   What patterns have you noticed in your life regarding the types of individuals that you tend to attract as friends, dating partners, and/or spouses?

_____

_____
_____
_____
_____
_____

3.   What patterns have you noticed regarding how friends, family, acquaintances, coworkers, etc. treat you, and how has their treatment affected the ways that you view and treat yourself?

_____
_____
_____
_____
_____

4.   Now, review your answers to the previous questions. Explain what they reveal about you, particularly what you can do to become more "self-protective."

_____
_____
_____
_____
_____

5.   What are the "Five Most Important Life Lessons" that you've learned, and how did you learn them?

_____
_____
_____
_____

Eight Important Life Lessons That I've Learned

In previous chapters, I shared some of the most "Important Life Lessons I've Learned." Here are eight others:

1. Forgetting my Core Beliefs, especially that I am God's child, was created in His image, and that I'm fearfully and wonderfully made will always cause problems for me.

2. I must always remember to protect my heart. One of my favorite scriptures says "Keep your heart with all diligence; for out of it are the issues of life" (Proverbs 4:23). As an empath, it's essential for me to remember to protect my heart from users, abusers, and predators who will give me a sob story, and then, try to take advantage of my kindheartedness.

3. "Blood isn't thicker than water." Many people are reared to believe that they should always be loyal to their blood relatives. I totally disagree with this notion. Most of our biggest sources of pain can come from relatives. Furthermore, children are more likely to be sexually abused by a blood relative, stepfather, or mother's boyfriend than by a stranger. When a family member has shown me that he or she is a "Mean Ole Girl" or "Snake-on-Two-Legs," I protect myself by keeping my distance from that individual as much as possible.

4. Being a good listener is a great self-protection strategy. As a naturally outgoing and friendly person who likes to help others, I tend to be very talkative. Because I'm invited to do lots of public speaking, being a "good talker" is necessary. However, over the years, I've learned that I often talk out of nervousness. This nervousness is actually a message from my "gut" (intuition, subconscious, and "funny feeling"), to warn me that I'm in the presence of a "Mean Ole Girl" or "Snake-on-Two-Legs." The same is true of emotional eating. When I eat rapidly, without tasting or enjoying my food while in someone else's presence, I've learned that my "gut" is trying to warn me to beware of that individual. Therefore, listening to what people say, in order to make sure that their words and actions are consistent, is important. But it's even more important for me to listen to what my intuition is trying to tell me.

5. Starting and ending each day well, is a powerful self-protection strategy. I once met a parent in Atlanta who told me that each day, she and other Black parents put a "Teflon Coat" on their children. She explained that they armed their children with positive affirmations and strategies (the "Teflon Coat") to help them ward off racism and other problems. Like those parents, I start each day by putting on my own "Teflon Coat." My coat consists of beginning my day on a positive note and ending it on a positive note. Before I leave home, (a) I listen to a motivational sermon by Joel Osteen, that I pre-record on my television; His sermons are loaded with uplifting advice about dealing with haters, fear, rejection, and low self-esteem; (b) While I'm drinking my home-made green smoothies and green tea, I read the Bible, Bible commentaries, and self-help books, especially books about nutrition and good health; (c) I pray, which includes thanking God for blessings, such as my health, family, and job, asking for wisdom and guidance for the day, and for protection from "mess, stress, and drama;" (d) I exercise for 20-30 minutes; (e) At bedtime, I also pray.

6. Seeking the approval of others will always backfire. Because of low self-esteem, a poor self-image, and rejection issues, I grew up believing that others looked better and were smarter than me. This caused me to become a very needy person. I often confided in the wrong people, and asked the wrong people for advice. I ended up learning the hard way, that "approval addiction" gave people who didn't have my best interests at heart power over me, and gave control freaks permission to take advantage of me. I could share many related stories, but will simply say that "learning to take my problems to God through prayer," and being extremely selective about whom I trust, have empowered me.

7. It's foolish to try to fit in with people and situations that are wrong for me.

8. Success is the best revenge.

The following section includes additional self-care and self-protection strategies that have been helpful to me.

Additional Self-Care and Self-Protection Strategies That Have Worked for Me

- I limit negative stimuli, such as news programs, and use ear plugs and ear muffs to drown out noise.
- I stopped reading True Crime books.
- I limit telephone calls and other types of conversations with users, abusers, negative individuals, and so-called "friends" who have a habit of dumping their problems on me, but not being available when I need to talk about a problem of my own.
- Instead of worrying, fearing, and spending too much time thinking about "frenemies," I keep their names and the names of the "Mean Ole Girls" and "Snakes-on-Two-Legs" who have personally harmed me, on a very special prayer list that I reserve for their kind. In other words, as bestselling author, pastor, and television evangelist Dr. Charles Stanley advises, "I have learned to fight every battle on my knees."
- I use deep breathing exercises to calm anxiety and alleviate stress.
- When I have trouble sleeping, I start counting my blessings.
- Instead of holding things inside, I've started to speak up more.
- Prayer, and "focusing on the size of my God, instead of the size of my problems" (as Joel Osteen and Dr. Stanley recommend) are great ways to alleviate worry.
- Walking at the beach and the zoo has a very calming effect on me.
- Watching the beautiful pink flamingos at the zoo, and watching

the hummingbirds, and beautiful yellow birds that fly into my backyard relax me.

- Instead of waiting for and expecting others to give me gifts, I buy birthday, Christmas, and Mother's Day gifts for myself.
- I sing and listen to some of my favorite gospel songs every day.
- Each morning, when I look in the mirror for the first time, I say "Good morning, Beautiful!" or "Hello Beautiful!"
- Before I get dressed and put on makeup, I take morning selfies while still in my pajamas, and say "Hello Beautiful! You are God's child!"
- At the end of his "Sweating to the Oldies" exercise videos, Richard Simmons use to say, "Now, give yourself a hug." I've learned the importance of giving myself a hug after exercising and accomplishing difficult tasks.
- Reading Cheryl Richardson's *The Art of Extreme Self-Care: Transform Your Life One Month at a Time*, was very helpful to me.

Personal Growth Exercise: Self-Care and Self-Protection (Part 3)

---

1.   How much time do you spend on "inner beauty self-care," and what specific "self-care" strategies do you engage in daily?

_____

_____

_____

_____

_____

_____

2.   What are your best "stress busters?"

_____

_____

_____

_____

_____

_____

3.   Who and what are the "joy snatchers" and "peace stealers" in your life? What is your action plan to protect yourself from them?

_____

_____

_____

_____

_____

_____

4.   One way to become more "self-protective," nurturing and kind to yourself, is to find places where you can pray, meditate, do deep breathing, and be at peace with yourself and the world. What are your favorite sanctuaries and places to find peace?

_____

_____

_____

_____

_____

_____

5.   If you were a bird, what type and color of bird would you be, and where would you fly if you could go anywhere you chose to go?

_____

_____

_____

_____

_____

6.   Make a list of your favorite uplifting songs that you can sing and listen to, in order to fight stress and improve your mood.

_____

_____

_____

_____

_____

_____

Becoming Your Own Best Friend

Earlier, I said that by the time that you reached the end of this chapter, my goal was for you to be closer to becoming your own best friend. Becoming your own closest friend is a great self-care and self-protection strategy that will help you progress on your *inner growth journey*. If you've reached the point where you truly accept and love yourself-- inwardly and outwardly--, enjoy your own company, enjoy being alone, behave in accordance with your Core Beliefs most of the time, and protect yourself from stressors, "Mean Ole Girls," and "Snakes-on-Two-Legs," you're probably there. Congratulations! If you aren't there yet, keep doing your best to get there.

GOD CREATED ME IN HIS IMAGE, AND I AM BEAUTIFUL.

I DESERVE TO PROTECT MYSELF.

I DESERVE TO TAKE GOOD CARE OF MYSELF!

Chapter Ten
Soaring Towards Your Destiny

Dear Beautiful!

Throughout my lifetime, I've had many "strikes" against me that could've caused me to become a negative statistic: incarcerated, drug addicted, an alcoholic, homeless, or dead prematurely as the result of a tragedy. My "strikes" included, growing up on Welfare, being abused, being viewed by teachers as a failure, having low self-esteem, and believing that I was ugly, inferior, and cursed. Furthermore, during the period when I was a single parent and on Welfare *again* as an adult, I became so depressed that I was actually planning to kill myself.

When people hear my personal story for the first time at a church, conference, school, or during a workshop that I'm conducting, I'm sure that they wonder how a woman who had so many "strikes" against her, could end up having such an amazing, blessed, and successful life. So, in this chapter, I share the "Secrets to My Success," and strategies to help you create your own "Roadmap to Success." This roadmap will help you *soar towards your destiny.* Your destiny is connected to your *inner growth journey*, especially your Core Beliefs about your purpose in life. Your purpose is the reason why you were put on this earth. Before we continue, I'd like for you to complete the next Personal Growth Exercise.

Personal Growth Exercise: Your Destiny (Part 1)

---

1.   What are the main "strikes" or problems that you've experienced?

_____

_____

_____

_____

_____

_____

2.   In your opinion, what are the main reasons why you were put on this earth, and why do you believe this?

_____

_____

_____

_____

_____

_____

The Secrets to My Success

"The Secrets to My Success" are three simple "ingredients": faith, hard work, and persistence. In a chapter of *Reaching the Mountaintop of the Academy: Personal Narratives, Advice, and Strategies From Black Distinguished and Endowed Professors*, I explained the reasons for my success in detail. Here's a summary of what I said about each of these three ingredients.[1]

Faith: The Main Ingredient

During childhood, I developed "a personal relationship with Jesus Christ by accepting Him as my Lord and Savior." This was the most important decision that I've ever made. However, during my college years and afterwards, I strayed from the foundational Christian principles that I'd been taught. I got pregnant by a man who promised to marry me, but when I was eight months pregnant, he informed me that he was marrying someone else. In order to survive financially, I had to go on Welfare.

After my baby was born, I moved to a different city, rented a room in the home of a "friend" and her husband, and began working as a substitute teacher. Substitute teaching allowed me to get off of Welfare, but I still could barely "make ends meet." In addition to not having my own place to live, I didn't have a car, a permanent job, or health care benefits. My sister, Tracy, was kind enough to loan me a used car, which enabled me to have transportation to and from work, without having to depend on that "friend" for a ride. But soon, a family tragedy occurred. On top of that, I became deathly ill from pneumonia-- without having medical coverage. Because of these circumstances, I "hit rock bottom": I became so depressed that I decided to kill myself.

One night, as I lay in bed next to my baby, trying to figure out the best way to end my life, I received a *God-sent message* from my subconscious: "Gail, *you know* there's a better way." Although I was weak from a lack of food and in pain from the pneumonia, I crawled out of bed, got on my knees, and began praying for help. As tears rolled down my face, I said, "God: If You will get me out of these people's house, I will serve you for the rest of my life!"

Three months later, my baby and I moved into our own government-subsidized-low-income apartment. A few months after that, I got a permanent teaching job. Soon, I returned to school and earned a Teaching Credential, and a Master's Degree. When my daughter was three years old, I married my husband, and we recently celebrated our Thirty-First Wedding Anniversary!

Since those horrible days long ago, I've repeatedly found that the God whom I serve "is able to do exceeding and abundantly above all that I can ask or think" (Ephesians 3:20). He has been faithful to me, and faith has been the main ingredient of my personal and professional success.

Hard Work: The Second Most Important Ingredient

I've been a hard worker all of my life. As a child, my mother required me to start washing dishes at age seven. During elementary school, I also had to comb my hair, and the hair of my two younger sisters before going to school. On weekends, before we could play, two of my sisters and I had to scrub walls, vacuum, and perform numerous chores. I also babysat neighborhood kids, and when I was in ninth grade, I even worked as a live-in-maid and caretaker for an invalid woman. That job only lasted for one week, because when my mother learned that I wouldn't be allowed to come home during the week, she insisted that I quit. During my high school years, I cleaned the home of one of our school vice principals on weekends, worked in a restaurant for a short time, and worked full time each summer.

If you'll recall, the results of the personality test that I shared previously, also showed that I work at "a faster than average pace." This has always been true. For example, during the period when I was a doctoral student, I was also a high school teacher, and taught part-time at two universities. In spite of this, through prayer and hard work, I earned my Ph.D. in two-and-a-half years, and received "The Dissertation of the Year Award." These are a few examples of how having a strong work ethic has contributed to my success.

Persistence: The Third Most Important Ingredient

Persistence, the third ingredient of my success, means that I don't give up easily, and will keep trying to accomplish my goals even when challenges arise. Let me share two examples. The first happened when I was a college undergraduate. The second occurred later, when I was trying to become a published writer.

As you know, I grew up on Welfare, and some teachers and family members viewed me as "dumb" for flunking first grade. In spite of this, through faith, hard work, and a sixth-grade teacher who helped me change my outlook, I not only graduated high school, but got accepted to several universities, and won several scholarships and grants.

Of the five universities that accepted me, I decided to attend the University of Southern California (USC) in Los Angeles. This private university had a great reputation and was considered to be very prestigious. When I arrived at the university, I had high hopes and dreamed of becoming a newspaper reporter. But my plans quickly went downhill.

Because I hadn't been adequately prepared for college during my junior high and high school years, I started my freshmen year of college with very weak academic skills, especially poor writing skills. As a result, I earned low grades in several of my university courses, so my grade point average fell. This caused a spiral effect.

First, I lost one of my grants, which required me to maintain a certain grade point average that I'd failed to keep. This meant that the only way that I could afford to remain at the university was to get a job. So, for the next few years, I worked part time during the school year, and full time each summer.

The second consequence was that the university "advisor" who had been assigned to work with me-- but had never contacted me before-- requested to meet with me. When I arrived at his office, this man didn't waste any time telling me three things: (1) that I would never be admitted into the School of Journalism; (2) that I'd never graduate from that university; and (3) that I needed to drop out of the university. I was shocked, embarrassed, and left his office in tears. As I headed back to my campus-owned apartment, I kept thinking how happy some of my haters in my hometown would be, when they learned that I'd been forced to drop out of the university.

When I reached my apartment, instead of packing my belongings in order to return to my hometown, I realized that the advisor was powerful, but he wasn't God! He was merely a man, and he didn't control my destiny. Then, I quickly got on my knees and began to pray for help. Through prayer, I received the answers that I needed. In *Reaching the Mountaintop of the Academy . . .* , here's how I explained those answers:

> I had to stop attending so many parties, stop attending so many athletic events, open up the grammar and composition book that had been assigned by my freshmen composition instructor (a book that I'd never opened), and do all of the exercises in that book! . . . In the end, thanks to that prayer, I literally taught myself how to write basic sentences, paragraphs, and essays. Consequently, over time, my grade point average improved. The best part is that four years after I enrolled in USC, I graduated on time, and on the Dean's Honor Roll![2]

The second example of the role of persistence in my success is directly related to the previous one, especially being forced to teach myself basic writing skills. Here's how I described it in *Reaching the Mountaintop of the Academy . . . .*:

> Another important lesson that I've learned is that rejection is inevitable, and since I've had my share of rejection, I've become an expert on this topic. I've been rejected by certain family members, former friends, colleagues, and others. Therefore, the main lesson that I've learned is "to keep it moving . . . ."
>
> For the past 20 years, I've also received hundreds of rejection letters from editors and publishers. During these times, I've given myself permission to feel disappointed and even angry, but not for long. Just as I refuse to let folks who reject me or dislike me, keep me from pursuing my goals, I've decided to keep writing, and to keep submitting my essays, book reviews, articles, book chapters, and book proposals, regardless of how many rejection letters I receive, because I strongly believe that "success is the best revenge," my opinions matter, and that my writing needs to be published.[3]

The bottom line is that if it weren't for the three main ingredients of my success-- faith, hard work, and persistence-- I would never have become the author of many *published* books, articles, book chapters, newspaper essays, book reviews, etc. The next Personal Growth Exercise is related to the previous sections.

Personal Growth Exercise: Your Destiny (Part 2)

---

1. What are your thoughts about the previous section?

_____

_____

_____

_____

2.   Have you ever felt like giving up on life? If so, what caused you to feel this way, and how did you handle the situation?

_____

_____

_____

_____

_____

_____

3.   When life becomes difficult, what strategies do you use in order to "keep moving forward?"

_____

_____

_____

_____

_____

_____

4.   How important is "faith" in your life, and how is it related to your Core Beliefs?

_____

_____

_____

_____

_____

_____

5.   How strong is your "work ethic," and what examples can you provide?

_____

_____

_____

_____

_____

_____

6.   How persistent are you, and what examples can you provide?

_____

_____

_____

_____

_____

How to Soar Towards Your Destiny

Soaring towards your destiny and living the life that you were created to live, require you to do two main things: (1) Identify your purpose(s), and (2) Plan for success, by creating a personalized roadmap. Let's begin that process!

Identifying Your Purpose(s)

In the first Personal Growth Exercise of this chapter, I asked you to explain the reasons why you were put on this earth. If you had trouble answering that question, don't worry. If someone had asked me that question during my childhood and many years later, I would've had trouble answering correctly. For example, when I was in elementary school, a man asked me what I wanted to be when I grew up. Even though my family was Pentecostal, instead of Catholic, I answered, "I want to become a nun!"

During high school, my dream was to become a news reporter, so, I went to college to earn a Journalism Degree, yet I ended up becoming a teacher. I taught junior high and high school for 14 years, before earning my doctorate and becoming a professor. I was a professor for nearly 20 years, before receiving a wonderful job offer in Corporate America, which is where I currently work.

In a previous chapter, I told you that after flunking first grade, I became an excessive talker at school, which caused me to get into a lot of trouble. But back then, no one-- including me-- realized that talking is one of my God-given talents. Although I wanted my late sister Tammie's quiet personality, and have *often* "put my foot in my mouth," said the wrong things, spoke without thinking things through, given unsolicited advice, talked too much, and not listened enough, I now know that God gave me the "gift of gab" for a reason: Talking is directly linked to my destiny: the reasons why I was placed on this earth. This gift has resulted in my receiving invitations to speak throughout the United States. The same is true of another one of my God-given gifts: writing.

If you'll recall, when I was a university student, my poor writing skills caused many problems for me. In spite of this, I've always been *driven* to write down my thoughts and feelings. For example, when I was in ninth grade and had no friends, I wrote a story about a girl who had no friends. Before I went to Africa, I wrote many stories that I tried to get published. While living in Africa, I kept a journal, and when I returned to the U.S., I wrote articles and stories about Africa that no one would publish. But because of my natural urge, I kept writing, even after receiving rejection letters for decades.

Nevertheless, like talking, my God-given writing talent has opened many professional "doors" for me. Countless individuals have read my published books, articles, and essays. Furthermore, one of my books, *The Power of One: How You Can Help or Harm African American Students*, was nominated for a national award, and *Through Ebony Eyes: What Teachers Need to Know but are Afraid to Ask About African American Students* motivated radio and television hosts to interview me.

Although I wanted to become a news reporter, and never wanted to become a teacher, when I look back over my life, it's clear that I was destined to be a teacher. For example, after flunking first grade, I use to teach a group of first graders everything they needed to know in order to be successful in first grade. In other words, I led a little clique in which I was the "teacher" and they were "my students." When I was in junior high school, I also taught Sunday School classes to younger children. When I was a single parent who was desperate to find ways to support my baby, getting a permanent teaching job was a lifesaver. However, it wasn't part of *my plan* for my life. Later, during my years as a professor, I trained teachers and school leaders, wrote books, and spoke to thousands of educators at schools and conferences. But when I first stand before educators to speak, the thing that they respect most is that I am a *former teacher*, who has "walked in their shoes." Today, as I look back on my professional career, the fact that my teaching ability is a gift from God, and part of the reason why He put me on this earth is obvious.

All of the jobs that I've had-- school teacher, university professor, and Equity and Professional Development Expert in Corporate America-- have required me to write, speak, and teach. In other words, my three strongest talents (gifts from God), teaching, writing, and motivational speaking, are connected to my purpose and destiny: I was *destined* to use my teaching, writing, and motivational speaking to empower others. So, one of the best ways for you to identify your purpose(s) is to figure out what your God-given talents are. Figuring this out will give you clues as to why you were put on this earth. The next Personal Growth Exercise will help you do this.

Personal Growth Exercise: Your Destiny (Part 3)

1.   What are your favorite hobbies?

_____

_____

_____

_____

_____

_____

2.   What activities are you "naturally" good at?

_____

_____

_____

_____

_____

3.   If you didn't have to "go to work or school" each day, how would you spend most of your time, and why?

_____

_____

_____

_____

_____

_____

4.   If you could create the perfect job for yourself, what would your job description consist of, and why would this be the perfect job for you?

_____

_____

_____

_____

_____

5.   Before you leave this earth, what are the main things that you would like to accomplish, and why?

_____

_____

_____

_____

_____

_____

6.　　Now, review your answers to the previous questions, and explain what you learned from them about your purpose(s) and destiny.

_____

_____

_____

_____

_____

Creating Your "Roadmap to Success"

As you can tell from the previous sections, my destiny wasn't clear to me until I was able to connect my God-given talents, strongest personality traits, events that occurred in my life, and the "doors of opportunity" that were opened to me. But the pattern is clear that _everything_ was connected, no matter what I thought. So, even if the reasons why _you_ were put on this earth aren't crystal clear to you, all of the Personal Growth Exercises that you've completed throughout this book, should give you answers that help you soar towards your destiny. Here are some additional suggestions:

- **Create a "My Roadmap to Success" journal.**
- **Decorate your journal.**
- **Add a Table of Contents.**
- **Complete the following exercises:**
- Make a list of your best personality traits.
- Write a paragraph that explains where you would like to be in 3 months, and how you plan to attain this goal.
- Write a paragraph that explains where you would like to be in 6

months, and how you plan to attain this goal.

- Write a paragraph that explains where you would like to be in 1 year, and how you plan to attain this goal.
- Write a paragraph that explains where you would like to be in 3 years, and how you plan to attain this goal.
- Write a paragraph that explains where you would like to be in 5 years, and how you plan to attain this goal.
- Write a paragraph that explains where you would like to be in 10 years, and how you plan to attain this goal.
- Write a paragraph that explains where you would like to be in 15 years, and how you plan to attain this goal.
- Write a paragraph that explains where you would like to be in 20 years, and explain how you plan to attain this goal.
- Create a list of Positive Affirmations about yourself, and include them in your journal.
- Read your Positive Affirmations at least once each week.
- Review and update your goals on a regular basis.
- Each month, write the goals that you've accomplished.
- Each month, review your progress and add your "Next Steps."

Reminders About Your Destiny

Regardless of what you've been told and what you've experienced, you can become the woman of your dreams. The following additional reminders should be helpful to you:

- **Keep your Core Beliefs in mind.**
- **Keep your "Roadmap to Success" in mind.**
- **Work hard.**
- **Keep learning, growing, and empowering yourself.**
- **Avoid negative people.**
- **Try not to get sidetracked or distracted.**
- **Surround yourself with supportive people.**
- **Keep believing that you can accomplish your goals.**
- **No matter what has happened to you in the past, make daily**

choices that will increase your chances of having a great future.

- Be willing to make sacrifices to attain your dreams.
- Start doing your homework early, by learning information that will enable you to become successful, such as viewing podcasts and reading articles and books that will move you closer to becoming an "expert" in your field.
- Do everything that you can to improve your reading, writing, and speaking skills.
- Try to find a good mentor.
- Be prepared for the haters, who will surface in unexpected places (including among family members, friends, coworkers, other students, etc.).
- Learn the words of the song "Sometimes You Have to Encourage Yourself," and on stressful days, keep singing it until you feel better.
- Listen to James Ingram's song "I Believe I Can Fly" periodically.
- No matter how successful you become, don't let it go to your head.
- Mentor and become a good role model to children from challenging backgrounds (in your family, neighborhood, church etc.).

I AM BEAUTIFUL BECAUSE I WAS CREATED IN GOD'S IMAGE.

I AM TALENTED, HAVE GREAT POTENTIAL, AND CAN ATTAIN MY GOALS.

I HAVE AN AMAZING DESTINY.

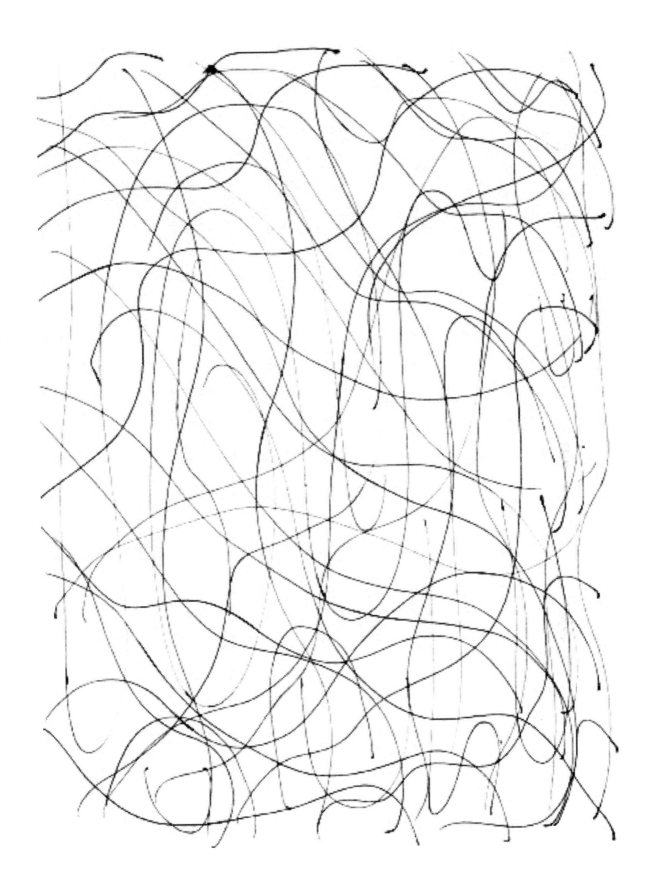

Conclusion
Connecting the Dots

Dear Beautiful!

Although we've reached the end of our journey together, I know that you'll continue to make progress on your personal *inner growth journey*, by striving to:

- accept,
- love,
- protect, and
- value

the *inwardly* and *outwardly* beautiful Black woman whom God created you to be.

I also believe that you'll keep soaring towards your destiny in order to fulfill your God-ordained purpose(s) on this earth. Please also remember to recite the Daily Affirmations, and share your thoughts about this book with me via email. I'm concluding with a final story, followed by Daily Affirmations and Art Therapy.

The Latina Mama Who "Got It Right"

In late 2017, my husband and I went to an amusement park with one of our daughters and two grandsons to celebrate the birthday of our eldest grandson, Iveren. Before we even reached the park, seven-year-old Iveren made it clear that the "Water Park" section was the only thing that he was interested in. And he kept his word. From the moment that we arrived at the park, he wasn't satisfied until we reached the area consisting of huge water slides, a river for canoeing, water fountains to play in, and roller coasters that plunged into a huge pond.

When we finally got to the "Water Park," while each adult took turns monitoring him, we let Iveren play to his heart's content. The "Water Park" was very crowded, and I noticed that several adults were spraying something from a can on children. Later, as I was eating lunch, a woman and little boy sat next to me. Then, the woman pulled a can out of a bag, and began to spray the boy.

I asked her how old he was, and what she was spraying on him. The woman said that her son was three years old, and that the item was "sunscreen." Then, the child, who was only wearing swim trunks, asked her *why* she was spraying him. The woman replied, "I think you are perfect now, and you'll look even better than you already do." The little boy giggled, and his mother smiled.

This scene was so moving to me that I quickly began to take notes about what I'd witnessed. I didn't want to forget the powerful lesson it conveyed. You see, the mother was a Latina, and her son was clearly biracial: half Black and half Latino. Obviously, she knew the type of discrimination that he would face as a result of being "mixed race" and having very dark skin. So, that day, this mother was doing two things: She was using literal sunscreen to protect his skin from sun damage; and she was already putting a "Psychological Teflon Coat" on him with her words. She wanted her son to understand that no matter what anyone else said, he was beautiful and "perfect" as he was. This "Psychological Teflon Coat" would make it easier for him to deal with racists, haters, "Mean Ole Girls/Boys," and "Snakes-on-Two-Legs" who could try to deceive him later.

As you continue on your *inner growth journey*, I hope that you will remember this story, and keep protecting yourself by "wearing" your own "Psychological Teflon Coat" each day. I look forward to hearing from you. Enjoy the final Daily Affirmations and Art Therapy.

I AM BEAUTIFUL BECAUSE I WAS CREATED IN GOD'S IMAGE.
I HAVE AN AMAZING AFRICAN ANCESTRY.
I LOVE MY PERSONALITY, SKIN TONE, HAIR TEXTURE, FEATURES, AND BODY.

I'M EXTREMELY
VALUABLE, AND
INTELLIGENT.
I DESERVE TO TAKE
GOOD CARE OF MYSELF.
I CAN ATTAIN MY GOALS.
I AM SOARING
TOWARDS MY DESTINY.

I WILL PUT MY TEFLON COAT ON DAILY IN ORDER TO REMEMBER WHO I AM, WHOSE I AM, AND IN ORDER TO PROTECT MYSELF FROM RACISTS, HATERS, MEAN OLE GIRLS/BOYS, AND SNAKES·ON·TWO·LEGS.

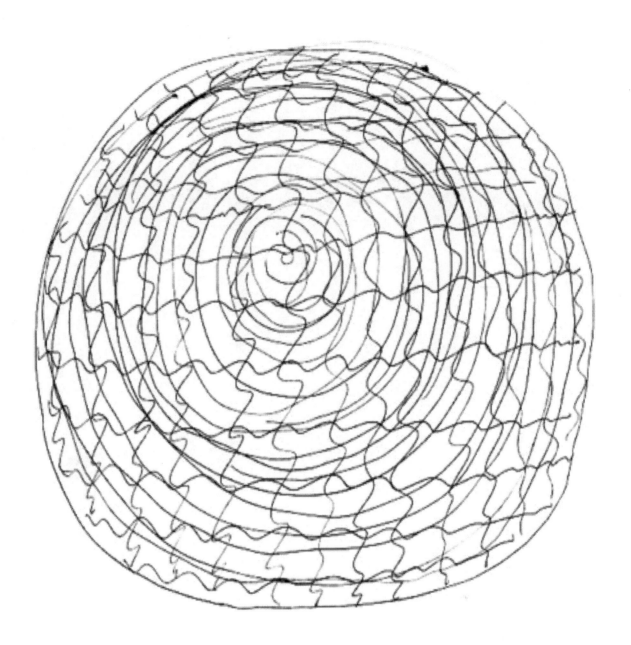

References

Chapter Two

1. Thompson, G. L. (2009). *A Brighter Day: How Parents Can Help African American Youth*. p. 45. Chicago: African American Images.

Chapter Three

1. Thompson, G. L. (2009). *A Brighter Day: How Parents Can Help African American Youth*. pp. 35-58. Chicago: African American Images.

Chapter Four

1. Kayla Lattimore. (NPR 2017). When Black Hair Violates the Dress Code. http://www.npr.org/sections/ed/2017/07/17/534448313/when-black-hair-violates-the-dress-code?utm_source=npr_newsletter&utm_medium=email&utm_content=20170723&utm_campaign=NPREd&utm_term=NPR_Ed

2. 13 Crazy Things White People Think About Black Natural Hair at Work and School. https://www.huffingtonpost.com/entry/13-crazy-things-white-people-think-about-black-natural_us_5762b327e4b057ac661b7780.

Chapter Five

1. Sara "Saartjie" Baartman. http://www.sahistory.org.za/people/sara-saartjie-baartman
2. "The significance of Sarah Baartman." http://www.bbc.com/news/magazine-35240987.
3. Sara "Saartjie" Baartman. http://www.sahistory.org.za/people/sara-saartjie-baartman
4. Ibid.
5. Ibid.
6. CDC. How Much Physical Activity Do Children Need? https://www.cdc.gov/physicalactivity/basics/children/index.htm
7. Mayo Clinic. How Much Should the Average Adult Exercise Every day? https://www.mayoclinic.org/healthy-lifestyle/fitness/expert-answers/exercise/faq-20057916

Chapter Eight

1. Thompson, G. L. (2009). *A Brighter Day: How Parents Can Help African American Youth*. Chicago: African American Images.

Chapter Nine

1. Light, A. (2016). *What Happened, Miss Simone? A Biography*. New York: Crown Publishing.
2. Aron. E. N. (1996). *The Highly Sensitive Person: How to Thrive When the World Overwhelms You*. New York: Harmony Books.
3. McGregor, J. & McGregor, T. (2013). *The Empathy Trap: Understanding Antisocial Personalities*. London: Sheldon Press.

Chapter Ten

1. Thompson, G. L., Bonner ll, F. A., & Lewis, C. W. (eds.) (2016). *Reaching the Mountaintop of the Academy: Personal Narratives, Advice, and Strategies From Black Distinguished and Endowed Professors*. Charlotte, NC: Information Age Publishing, Inc.
2. Ibid. p. 116.
3. Ibid. p. 118.

Made in the USA
San Bernardino, CA
06 January 2018